POWER LIVING

POWER LIVING

MASTERING THE ART
OF
SELF-DISCIPLINE

Michael Anthony Janke

Special Operations Publishing

Virginia Beach, VA

Dedicated to my beautiful wife Athena, for her endless support, love, guidance, and inspiration. She is truly the pilot of my destiny.

For my wife.

Other fine books and tapes by the author are available from www.specopsconsulting.com

Library of Congress Cataloging-in-Publication Data
Janke, Michael Anthony
     Power Living: Mastering The Art of Self-Discipline / Michael Anthony Janke
     p. cm.
     Includes bibliographical references and index
     Preassigned LCCN : 99-91240
     ISBN : 0-9675139-3-6
     1. Self-control. 2. Success-Psychological aspects. 3. Self-containment.(Personality trait)
     I. Title

     BJ1533.D49J36 1999   179'. 9
                    QBI99-901711

Edited by Kathleen Marusak

ATTENTION ORGANIZATIONS, CORPORATIONS, ASSOCIATIONS AND SCHOOLS OR LEARNING CENTERS:
Quantity discounts are available on bulk purchases of this book for educational purposes or fund raising. Special books or book excerpts can also be created to fit specific needs. For information on how to order this book or audio tape cassettes in bulk, or to book Mr. Janke to speak at your next meeting, please contact C.D.Lilly, Inc, 24195 Juanita Dr, Quail Valley, CA 92587 or call (877) 625-2653.

Books by Michael A. Janke

Power Living
Becoming SuperHuman

Audiotapes by Michael A. Janke

Mastering Self-Discipline (2-tape audio series)
Becoming SuperHuman: The Dynamic Laws of Personal
Achievement (2-tape audio series)

HOW TO CONTACT THE AUTHOR

Michael Anthony Janke is a Navy SEAL commando, professional
speaker, and consultant to Fortune 500 companies from around the
world. Requests for information about having the author speak at
your next meeting or convention, as well as information about
Special Operations Consulting, should be directed to the address
below. Readers of this book are also encouraged to contact the
author with comments or suggestions.

C.D. Lilly, Inc.
In care of Michael A. Janke
24195 Juanita Drive
Quail Valley, CA 92587
1-800-543-2360

Web site: http://www.specopsconsulting.com

TABLE OF CONTENTS

List of Illustrations
About the Author
Preface
Foreword
Introduction

ABOUT THE AUTHOR

Michael Anthony Janke

 Michael Anthony Janke is a professional speaker, author, and founder of Special Operations Consulting. Mike has over 12 years of experience as a Navy SEAL Team commando, and is an internationally recognized expert on the topics of self-discipline, teamwork, and individual performance. Each year, Mike helps literally tens-of-thousands of people improve their lives through his books, audiotapes, and speaking presentations.

Michael Janke was born and raised on a small farm in the mountains of Northwestern Pennsylvania. It was from this humble beginning that he first came to know discipline as a force in life. After studying Ancient Philosophy at the University of Pittsburgh, he joined the Navy after hearing tales of adventure in a small and highly secretive unit called the SEAL Teams. Having a background in survival, martial arts, and collegiate sports, the SEAL's seemed like a perfect match.

In today's age of rapid change, high stress business, increasing technology, and global economies, Mike teaches people how to gain control of their hectic lives and stay focused on enjoying life. With the strong support of his loving wife Athena, Mike continues to help people from all walks of life discover a more disciplined way of living. Mike is the founder of Special Operations Consulting in Virginia Beach, Virginia.

Any questions or inquiries about Special Operations Consulting, Mike's books, tapes, or speaking schedule, can be sent to C.D.Lilly, Inc. 24195 Juanita Drive, Quail Valley, CA 92587 (800) 543-2360 or e-mail Mike through his web site at: http://www.specopsconsulting.com

LIST OF ILLUSTRATIONS

PREFACE

This Revolutionary Book Will Change Your Life!

Every human being has the potential to take control of their life. We all have the power to achieve great things and live a life full of pleasure, accomplishment, and purpose. For most people, this power is sleeping deep inside, waiting to be discovered and unleashed. In this book I have taken techniques, information, and simple tools from more than 12 years of experience with the elite U.S. Navy SEAL Teams, and combined them into a system that unlocks this power. This book is designed to be an instruction manual for the human animal known as man. It is imperative to understand that the first step to gaining control of your life is to have the desire to change. My intent is not to bog you down with theories of psychology, but rather to take you on a journey of self-discovery. As a Navy SEAL, I have been taught and practiced the techniques to overcoming my inherent weaknesses in body and mind, by nurturing and implementing the wonderful power of self-discipline.

This book is a simple instruction manual to controlling and fixing little glitches that have been built into the human machine. When reading this book, I want you to keep in mind that every human machine is built differently in size, ability, and life span. This book will introduce you to a time-proven format of positive change that is utilized in the special operations world to create men from mice and leaders from sheep. When you discipline your mind, body, and character, your life takes on a powerful force that accomplishes things you never thought possible. This book will provide you with all the tools you will need to control and shape the destiny you desire.

INTRODUCTION

The term discipline in today's world is almost non-existent. In this age of technology, pleasure, and instant satisfaction, we have more options and opportunities to experience anything we want whenever we want. Throughout childhood and into our late teenage years we live a life of set rules, regulations, and little responsibility. The consequences of doing wrong is set and enforced by our parents or guardian figure. In today's society of single parent families, and a national divorce rate of nearly 60%, we cannot realistically say that discipline is successfully taught or utilized to the extent that it was 25 or 50 years ago. If you have trouble believing this, just open up your local newspaper or turn on your television and view the types of crimes being committed and the age of the offenders.

School shootings are up, movie and television violence is everywhere, society is fatter, divorce is up, patriotism and chivalry are dead, sexual crimes are rampant and responsibility is shirked as quickly as we can "surf the web." Self- discipline is not merely a word, but a concept of behavior, actions, known facts, and set guidelines that we use to control the environment we live in. When we do not apply this control measure to our lives, we open ourselves up to habits, addictions, disease, financial ruin, and ultimately death. We now possess the abilities to cure disease, travel anywhere overnight, explore the universe, and live a life of pleasure, but with these new-found freedoms come more choices.

Personal discipline is nothing more than a fancy way of saying human will. The will to say yes and no. The will to do right and wrong, and the will to have control or not. Human will can be simplified further to mean actions and decisions that are made from the time we wake up to the time we go to bed, determining the outcome of our life. Self-discipline is the key to controlling all aspects of living that determine the quality and length of our existence on this planet. When a person is able to maximize the happiness, health, wealth, and vitality that occurs during his time alive on Earth, that person is not merely living, but **Power Living.**

In today's society, having a stress-filled daily schedule is normal to most people. It seems that we have a million things to do and only a short time in which to do them. Most people want to improve their health, relationships, financial state, and quality of life, but fail to realize that the answer lies within. Today, people turn to alcohol, drugs, television, and a variety of other avenues to hide from this dilemma. Since we live in a time where almost any behavior or action is acceptable, it has become even harder to maintain a disciplined lifestyle.

When you begin to accept the fact that you have total control over your thoughts, words, and actions, you can begin to learn to control them with self-discipline. I won't begin to insult your intelligence by stating that I have the answers to all of your problems, but I can tell you that all of your dreams, desires, and goals can easily be attained if you decide to develop the power of self-discipline. I urge you to break free from the prison of excuses and procrastination. Step up to the plate and become determined to take control of your life. Be willing to break out of your daily comfort cycle and take a step towards changing the little things. Life is just too short of a commodity to waste on excuses. Do yourself, your family, and your co-workers a favor by using the information found in this book to begin power living.

M.A. Janke

CHAPTER 1 - THE POWER OF DISCIPLINE

"If one in a thousand men is found to have strong discipline, he must be slain –for he has attained the skill of commanding his destiny –to which end, nothing is beyond his grasp."

-Ghingas Khan

As the sweat rolling off their foreheads and eyebrows falls noiselessly to the deck of the c-141 aircraft, large, well-muscled men quickly climb into their wetsuits. In the aircraft, flying at an altitude of 35,000 feet over the North Atlantic, several aircraft crew members stare curiously at these twelve men dressing in special black wetsuits with strange looking weapons and equipment. The quiet, easygoing demeanor of these strange men almost conceals the glowing confidence and cold determination that shows in their eyes. After nearly 13 hours of monotony, a voice booms out "15 minutes!" and the twelve men suddenly come to life.

Oxygen cylinders are checked, freefall parachutes are donned, and fins are taped to legs in preparation for the HALO, or high-altitude-low-opening jump. Each of the men has a partner, or swim-buddy, to whom they give all of their attention; checking straps, ripcords, weapons, night vision goggles, and small water-proof rucksacks. Viewing these men is like watching a precision machine at work. In a few minutes the methodical dance is over and the men slowly make their way to the rear of the aircraft.

Suddenly a little red light appears and a loud hum begins as the plane's ramp is lowered to reveal the beautiful loneliness of space. The dark and cold quickly engulf the inside of the aircraft as the –40 degrees Fahrenheit of altitude rushes in to meet the twelve men. Calmly staring out into the blackness, you can make out the reflection of the moon shining on the surface of the restless North Atlantic, and barely see the tiny speckles of light that make out the division between land and sea. You can feel the adrenaline pulsing in these twelve men as the red light suddenly turns green and the lead man reaches out with his hand, points into space, and yells – "GO!" The figures leap in unison like strange shadows into the night and disappear so fast you think your eyes are playing tricks on you. As the relative wind violently sweeps them from the sky, the group settles into a small twelve-man circle as they reach terminal velocity. Quick glances at the altimeters on their wrists tell the tale of gravity, 10,0000 ft, 9,000 ft, 8,000 ft. Falling at the rate of one thousand feet for every five seconds, they move closer and closer to Mother Earth.

After falling nearly 30,000 feet from the atmosphere, the group waves off and turns 180 degrees into the tracking position. This position accelerates them to almost 200mph and shoots them horizontally across the sky to provide opening separation for their ram-air parachutes.

Suddenly, there are twelve tiny parachutes maneuvering in the night sky. While under canopy, the air rushes up to provide a forewarning of the cold, dark, water below. The twelve men don their fins and activate the oxygen cylinders on their Draager underwater re-breathers.

Quickly, the ocean rushes up to meet them, as twelve splashes herald the inevitable shock of the freezing cold waters. Immediately upon entering the water, the men slip out of their parachutes and dive under the surface to gather in a small group under the churning surface of the great ocean. Once under the water, signals are passed, timers are set, and the electronic compass is activated. The group kicks out on a pre-determined compass bearing while maintaining a small V-shaped formation. The men must now discipline their bodies and minds to dismiss the freezing cold and surrounding darkness of the great ocean.

Several hours later, a single head slowly breaks the surface of the calm bay waters 500 yards behind the large and rusting Pakistani freight ship, and quickly disappears again below the surface. As the twelve men feel their way over the sea-life covered bottom of the ship, they stop at the huge 45-foot rudder that looms over them like a large house. Each man quickly takes off his Draager pure-oxygen re-breather, dive belt, fins, and hooks them unto a line suspended from the ship's hull by powerful magnets. Their MP-5 Heckler and Koch miniature machine-guns are unfastened and readied for use in the dark shadows behind the rusting vessel. Slowly and methodically, with guns pointed outward in a 360-degree circle, the men extend a retractable pole outfitted with a rubber-coated titanium hook. As the hook quietly grabs hold of a railing, the pole is retracted and slowly sunk to the bottom. The men patiently wait for the water to drain off of their bodies before climbing higher onto the back of the ship, by means of a lightweight wire-ladder.

The first couple of men reach the top of the ship's railing and flip down their night-vision goggles to scan the shadows of the ship's deck for terrorists. As the last man reaches the cover of the shadows, a faint almost inaudible sound is heard, followed by the faint smell of gunpowder drifting from the barrel of a silencer. The terrorist quietly crumples to the deck of the ship with the butt of his cigarette still glowing between his lips. Suddenly, the twelve shadows spring into action as if on cue, flowing over the ship like a violent and powerful wave of death. Surprise, speed, and disciplined violence are the tools these twelve surgeons use to bring justice to the unsuspecting soldiers of terrorism.

The sounds of the cold North Atlantic wind howling outside the crew's hatch remind the tall Iranian of his far-away homeland. Nervously, he lights a thick, Turkish cigarette as he glares at the helpless crew of the ship. Suddenly, with a rush of cold air, the hatch flies open to reveal a slender cylinder of steel only inches from his face, and in an instant, everything goes dark.

In minutes, the soldiers of terrorism no longer exist and the sounds of sirens can be heard off in the distance. Quickly, the twelve men gather on the aft deck of the ship. A small satellite beacon is activated as the men climb back into the cold bay waters. Twenty minutes later, the extraction is completed as the last man climbs down the bridge ladder of the U.S. nuclear submarine.

Back at the underground Special Operations Center in Washington DC, a sigh of relief is heard as the satellite receiver intercepts the signal of "mission accomplished-zero problems". As the morning sun rises over the East Coast of the United States, the inhabitants of this free nation wake up to another day of freedom, given to them by these twelve masters of self-discipline.

REALITY

*"When a man lacks discrimination and his mind is
undisciplined, his senses run hither and thither like wild
horses, but they obey the reins like trained horses when
he has self-discipline and his mind is one-pointed."
-Upanishads (800 B.C.)*

This story sounds like a Hollywood movie, or an excerpt from a Tom
Clancy novel, but in reality is just another day at the office for a group of
men called Navy SEALs. SEAL is an acronym for America's top secret,
and highly trained special operations unit, and stands for sea, air, and
land. Navy SEALs represent the modern version of the Samurai warriors
of ancient times, and stand as the ultimate consequence against
undisciplined decision making. Yes, even a terrorist must have discipline
in order to survive. It is due to their lack of discipline that these
individuals and organizations make poor tactical decisions in the quest to
further their cause.

Just as you and I faced consequences as a child when we broke
our parents pre-defined set of rules and regulations, so must these
individuals and organizations when they break our nation's stated
international guidelines of proper conduct. If we dissect this simple story
of actions, pre-determined rules, and set consequences further, we find a
fascinating parallel to our lives. On one hand, we have a highly dedicated
individual that has learned to discipline his body and mind in all
extremes, stresses, and conditions. On the other hand, we have an
undisciplined individual that chooses to ignore the information of good
and bad, right and wrong, and personal responsibility for personal action.

A similar scenario is played out every day in life. On one side, we have a 35-year-old father of two, who is a respected and reliable worker for an average manufacturing firm. On the other side, we have a 35-year-old divorced father of two, who is a despised and mistrusted worker that is fired from every job he has held. The first man is always up early, exercises daily, eats conscientiously and has a loving and respectful relationship with his family. This man treats everyone with respect and dignity, dresses neatly, and always gives 100% at work and at home everyday. He is not wealthy by any means, but budgets wisely and takes extra care of his family's possessions. He sets high standards of conduct and performance for himself and lives a healthy, satisfying, and virtually stress free life.

The second man is late to work two or three times a week, never exercises, eats whatever he wants and craves, always looks like he sleeps in his clothes, showers every other day, and appears unshaven and sloppy. He has been divorced twice due to his drinking, smoking, and selfish attitude in relationships. He blames everyone for his troubles except himself, and doesn't care to be a father to his children. This man never has money and is always on the verge of bankruptcy. His co-workers distrust him and his superiors would never place him in a position of responsibility. Because of his drinking and eating habits, he has a large beer belly that protrudes over his belt and is always unhappy with his life. When asked, he says he has bad luck with work, women, and money. He never accepts responsibility for anything in his life and believes that the world owes him a better living.

For the sake of discussion, let's assume that both men were raised by the same parents in the same household, and lived by the same set of rules and consequences. Upon departing the cocooned world of their parents, they both adopted their own set of rules and regulations. What factor determines the outcome of this story? Is it genetics, religion, or just fate? It is none of these, but simply and clearly <u>self-imposed discipline and human will.</u> Self-discipline is the foundation and key to a life of health, success, and vitality.

Personal discipline is responsible for turning around countries, economies, wars, and personal lives virtually overnight. In the SEAL Teams, we use many tactics and techniques that are based upon human behavior and human nature to control our actions. One technique or tactic that is responsible for a lot of our success in combat, is simply referred to as "The path least traveled." This technique is based upon the human tendency to go the easy route, or take the path of least resistance to make situations more pleasant for oneself. When we plan a route through a country or city, we find the most horrible, difficult, thickest, nastiest, and unpleasant location in and around our area of operation. We find the steepest cliff, the thickest swamp, the most run-down area of a city, or the most impassable terrain available and use it to our advantage.

This concept appears in everyday life of the majority of people today. The overweight person that knows he should not eat high fat and high cholesterol foods, chooses the path of least resistance by eating at a fast food restaurant instead of making a light and healthy lunch the night before. The person who would rather sit on the couch all day than do maintenance on his house or vehicles, or use his time wisely to better his life, is an example of this concept.

The technique of choosing the path least traveled is not one of self-martyrdom, or a decision to do things the hard way. Rather, one of identifying and correcting personal actions and thoughts to improve our performance in all aspects of daily life. This is accomplished by programming your mind to use discipline during decision-making to help ensure the choices we make in everyday life are of the greatest benefit, and not necessarily the easy way out.

Power living is the process of disciplining our thoughts and behaviors to maximize the amount of success, health, and vitality we experience in our short life span. Self-discipline can be further defined as a measure of one's will power and conscious effort to better one's body, mind, and spirit. We have a saying in the Teams for when the environment is at its worst, and we use this saying to remind us of our need to apply personal discipline when we need it the most. This simple saying of "Get what you need!", is said to remind each other of our inherent human tendency to take the path of least resistance in a time of decision-making.

When we decide to conduct our operations in the harshest of environment and location, we understand that this decision actually saves our lives and the lives of the people we are there to rescue. The consequences of operating without discipline are a known and proven fact, therefore we implement self-discipline into our lives to ensure our success and survival. By sacrificing in one small area of our personal comfort, we benefit in all other areas of our lives.

This simple technique can be used in every aspect of a person's life to increase the overall quality of their existence. For example, let's say you decide to take control of your life by budgeting a little more time and money for your appearance and clothing for work. You have sacrificed in one small area, but gain a respectful, clean, competent, and disciplined look and attitude. Another example of this technique can be used for your personal management skills. If you have a job that requires you to work in an office setting with a 9 to 5 schedule, chances are that you probably go with your co-workers out to lunch everyday. When you discipline yourself to make a healthy, balanced, and fat-free meal the night before, you not only save about $75 a week, but give yourself more personal quiet time to work on your future goals, or to exercise. This small, yet simple change, has not really caused you to sacrifice a whole lot, but has created a substantial benefit to your health, finances, and knowledge. When you add self-discipline into your life, you not only change your life, but the lives of everyone around you.

The changes you make in your life to improve your overall personal health, appearance, diet, and energy levels are accomplished by simply adding small amounts of discipline over a scheduled length of time. These moderate changes elevate your work performance, family life, financial stability, and general mental and physical health to powerful new levels. Most of us understand this concept by the time we reach adulthood, but somewhere along the way we get caught up in the schedule of life. As life becomes a routine occurrence instead of a journey of self-discovery, we tend to lose our personal set of rules and regulations little by little. This technique of understanding our built-in tendency to choose the path of least resistance instead of the path of greater value, allows us to gain clarity during the decision-making process.

The ability to choose what is better for us, instead of what is easier on us, comes from the process of building up our self-discipline or will power one step at a time. This technique is the foundation of powerful concepts that are implanted into our mind, and used when the decision-making process is begun. The object of this technique is to provide a thought pattern that first, and foremost, begins by controlling the human tendency to take the path of least resistance. When we have the ability to look at our choices in life and make our decisions based upon our own personal guidelines and rules, instead of instant satisfaction and immediate pleasure, we have begun to master discipline.

In today's age of incredible technology and scientific wonders, there exist so many opportunities, lifestyles, and directions for a person to choose from that our chances of making wrong decisions are dramatically increased. As with anything in life there is good and bad in all things.

Without an organized set of clear-cut goals, needs, desires, and aspirations, it becomes very hard to determine exactly what options in life you have to choose from. To simplify this subject further, we must first determine what it is we want in life, and exactly what outcome we desire.

To give you a simple example, imagine that your wife, husband, or significant other sends you to a huge multi-product store like Wal-Mart or Super K-mart. However, upon arrival you cannot remember what it is you were supposed to buy. In this super-store you have millions of items and products to choose from, so you walk around endlessly trying to figure out what you want. By the end of the day, you have seen only a 10th of what this super-store has to offer, but still have not found what you are looking for. This is much like most people in life, who have a thousand different choices each day of their lives and seemingly spend all day frantically doing nothing. This is because they have not yet found what it is they want, or what it takes to get it.

When I made the decision that I wanted to become a Navy SEAL, I found out that there was a set order of tasks, accomplishments, guidelines, and steps that I needed to follow in order to reach my goal. The human mind needs to have a set task and schedule to follow in order to focus its power. However, without a clear direction to follow, it starts to download glitches. The computer in your head is much like the computer you have at home or at work. In order to work efficiently and correctly, it needs a program or set order of guidelines to follow. Without this program of guidelines, it becomes nothing more than a useless box of information that continually spins its circuits and chips while accomplishing nothing.

The first step to mastering discipline is a basic and simple one, but for most people it is the hardest to pin down. The first step is to determine what it is we want in life, or what we want to become. I am not saying you need to determine that you want to be an astronaut or any other type of professional. Rather, we need to dig through our brain and come up with a general idea of the way we want things to be. All of this information is in there just waiting to be discovered.

Everyday we think, see, dream, and desire things in life. The problem is, we are unable to consciously focus and organize our efforts towards attaining them. The first, and most crucial step to bringing discipline into our lives, is accomplished by determining exactly what we want in our short existence. In today's world, there are so many experts and therapists telling you to get in touch with your feelings and to just let things happen, that people get even more confused about what actions to take. The truth is that you do not need to repeat a special chant, or pay thousands of dollars for a therapist to find clarity in your life. By discovering what your goals in life are, and focusing your time and energy towards them, your life takes on clarity and purpose.

Think of me as your personal Navy SEAL instructor, giving you a set order of instructions to follow. These instructions are designed to tremendously enhance your body, mind, and quality of life. The consequences for not following these instructions are already evident in our daily lives. If changes are not made now, you will die never having accomplished anything worthwhile and wasted the most valuable commodity of all, time. If all of this sounds a little harsh or demanding to you, remember that anything worth having in life is worth fighting for! The first step to power living is not accomplished by complacency, but rather by action, personal mastery, and self-discipline.

I am going to walk side-by-side with you in this journey through the process of mastering discipline and achieving a life of power. The missions that I have given you to accomplish after each chapter are based upon techniques and tactics we use in the SEAL Teams and the special operations world. Each mission is a small step in the journey to a life of success, happiness, and longevity. My role as your personal Navy SEAL instructor is to help you discover the hidden path that leads to a life of power living and vitality. Each of our paths are different in length and direction. It is up to you to determine the start and finish lines. Make today your starting line, and all that you desire as your finish line. Welcome to the world of self-discipline and power living!

SECRETS OF SELF-DISCIPLINE

"The best man in his dwelling loves the Earth. In his heart, he loves what is profound. In his associations, he loves humanity. In his words, he loves faithfulness. In government, he loves order. In handling affairs, he loves competence. In his activities, he loves timeliness. It is because he knows discipline that he is without reproach."
-Lao-Tzu (600 B.C)

Throughout history, successful people have had one obvious thing in common: personal discipline. High achievers are always willing to do things that average humans are unwilling to do. Self-discipline is not related to punishment. It is pure, sustained self-control. From recorded history, self-discipline has been responsible for the improvement of all mankind. Self-discipline has enabled scholars to discover breakthroughs in medicine, chemistry, physics, computers, and all other fields. Self-discipline has empowered warriors with the ability to fight against oppression and for freedom. It has blessed artists, writers, composers, and musicians with the persistence to complete beautiful works of art. It has elevated athletes to the top of their sports. It has allowed average men and women to overcome tremendous obstacles in their personal journeys to happiness, wealth, and success. It builds character, self-esteem, morals, courage, and honor in everyday people.

The achievement of anything of value requires personal discipline. It is painfully obvious that the majority of humans are living lives that are seriously lacking in self-discipline. A lack of self-discipline causes many problems, not only in our personal lives, but also in our homes, schools, jobs, and communities. Self-discipline is the ability to regulate your conduct by principal, persistence, and sound judgment rather than by desire, or social acceptance. Ninety-nine percent of the people on this planet don't know how to control themselves. They do whatever they feel like doing without remorse, responsibility, or concern over consequences. Contemporary American society, and most of the world, has lost sight of the need for self-control and self-discipline. How often have you heard people say, "I just don't have the time to work out today, maybe tomorrow", "I can't help being fat, its genetics", or "Why should I be on time, they don't pay me enough".

The disciplined person sets goals. He or she is living a life of self-discipline and control for the purpose of reaching his daily, monthly, yearly, and lifelong goals. Average humans don't set daily goals, they just live from day to day and complain about how unfair life is. The self-disciplined super-human moves deliberately each day toward something specific. What are your everyday and lifelong goals?

We cannot expect success and true happiness without building each aspect of our lives with self-discipline, control, and integrity. No one can have anything of lasting value without personal discipline. Self-discipline is the backbone of a successful, happy, and long life. Personal discipline brings prosperity, honor, strong character, and freedom into our lives.

It is through self-discipline that we set an example for our children, spouses, co-workers, and all others to see and admire. It is the essence of our character and the result of our thoughts, actions, and words. Learning effective discipline can set you free and reward you beyond your wildest dreams. At one time or another in your life, you have probably experienced the freedom and pride that comes from self-discipline. When you inject discipline, self-control, and persistence into your daily life, you open the door to a realm of limitless achievement and power.

SEVEN GOLDEN TRAITS OF SELF-DISCIPLINE

"To know and to act are one in the same".
-Samurai maxim

1. **Successful Time Management.** If you cannot control how you spend your time, you can be sure that people and circumstances will control it for you!

2. **Mastering Moods.** Disciplined people live by their commitments and goals, and not by their emotions and habits. Controlling how you act and react is the result of emotional discipline.

3. **Master Your Mouth.** Disciplined people understand that what comes out of their mouths is a direct reflection of who they are and what they are. Think about what you want to say, before you say it. Master verbal discipline.

4. **Physical Discipline.** Successful and dynamic people place a high priority on health and exercise, which enables them to accomplish more and enjoy their achievements longer.

5. **Financial Discipline.** The disciplined person knows the value of control and budgeting. The value of financial discipline is that it directs your money where you want it to go, rather than leaving you wondering where it went.

6. **Perception Control.** The high-achiever knows that his or her outward appearance is an advertisement to the world that says, " this is who I am, this is how neat and competent I am, come and see how disciplined I am." Control how other people perceive you by taking pride in your outward appearance.

7. **Character Strength.** Disciplined people are always looking to improve their character and personality. Super-Humans exploit their strong character traits, and demolish their weak habits. Start noticing what is weak in you, and begin enhancing what is strong in you.

What areas of your life are missing self-discipline? How often do you choose to the easy way out? What habits and traits do you possess that have more control over you than you have over them? The disciplines you establish today will determine your health, wealth, and success tomorrow. Do you remember the age-old saying that "nobody's perfect"? All humans have faults, bad habits, and character flaws, but the Super-Human uses self-discipline to reduce his or her flaws and stand above the average human. Developing self-discipline is not the act of punishment, total restriction, self-inflicted pain, or behaving like a robot. Self-discipline is a tool that each of us possesses to exact control over how we act, think, speak, and live, but the less we use of it, the more out of control our lives become.

Throughout our childhood years, we have all been exposed to discipline in one form or another. Discipline is often associated with punishment, being grounded, or doing something that you were forced to do. A child who has been punished unjustly or extremely, will most likely react by avoiding discipline in his or her adult life. A child who has been spoiled or over-indulged will most likely shun discipline as an adult. A child who experiences undisciplined adults will be programmed to live life with the same undisciplined attitude. This chain reaction of uncontrolled behavior and values can be reversed and overcome, simply by the desire and want for a better life. Every human being has been exposed to discipline as a child, perhaps by too much discipline, too little discipline, unbalanced discipline, or the wrong kind of discipline. It is up to us to reflect upon our daily performance, and reflect upon the problems within ourselves.

If we take a look at the past and present history of human societies, we can clearly see the use of mass discipline systems to exert control over the actions, words, and thoughts of populations. In today's society, the military uses regimented and restrictive living to discipline soldiers. Religion uses promises of heaven and hell to discipline the actions of billions of people. Countries use laws to discipline their populations. The need for control and discipline is a fact of human nature, but we can learn to master personal discipline to greatly enhance the quality of our own lives.

How do you develop self-discipline? In the SEAL Teams, each and every SEAL is personally responsible for his everyday performance and actions. By giving highly motivated and intelligent people the necessary information and environment to better themselves, you create a chain reaction of superior performance through self-discipline. If you place people who do not want to change in this environment, you get chaos, defiance, and poor performance. The two components that are found among highly successful people, like the Navy SEALs, is motivation and desire. How can you begin exerting control over your life if you don't care to do so in the first place?

The power and influence of personal discipline is wonderfully expressed in this simple story, first told to me by a poor fisherman in the tiny Amazon village of Iquitos, Peru. In ancient times, a poor farmer tried year after year to grow crops on a little spit of land in the fertile jungle.

Every year he would plant his crops and return to find them eaten and withered away. The poor farmer was very depressed because without a good crop, he would never be able to get married and have children. One day the poor farmer went up to the monastery on the hill to seek advice from the wise old Monks. After hearing his tale of sorrow, a wise old Monk agreed to help him grow the most prized crop of all – self-discipline. The Monk took the farmer out into the vast desert, where he placed a small seed in his hand and told him he must water it three times a day. The Monk told him that this was the seed of self-discipline, and only by watering it three times a day would he see the fruit of self-discipline.

Day after day, year after year, the poor farmer traveled a great distance, three times a day, to water the small seed. Eventually, the small seed grew into a large tree that bore sweet figs and provided lots of shade for other crops. The farmer was able to build a small house in the shade of this tree and sell his crops, eventually enabling him to afford a wife and children. Each year the farmer would bring a handful of figs to the Monk and ask him if this was the fruit of self-discipline, and each year the Monk would shake his head and reply "No".

Finally, after years of frustration, the farmer yelled at the Monk in anger and told him that no such fruit existed and that he had deceived him. The wise old monk replied, "You have successfully farmed the fruit of self-discipline, my son. You have become healthy, wealthy, and wise from this fruit, but you can never sell it or give it away. All you have desired has come true by planting the priceless seed of self-discipline in the rich soil of desire and motivation."

This short story is very much like most people today. We continually work day after day in the rich fields of life, never controlling and focusing our efforts on any specific goal, and never realizing the priceless seed of self-discipline we keep in our pockets. The good news is that most human beings have desire and motivation, but just need a little push in the right direction. That push comes from personal control and self-discipline.

Throughout this chapter you will learn many powerful techniques to help you understand and develop the self-discipline that is fast asleep inside you, waiting to be unleashed and experienced. It is very important that you understand the ingredients of desire and motivation, for without these you will never experience self-discipline. For example, if you truly hate working for somebody else, you will never accomplish Super-Human performance at this job. The best you can hope for is forced labor, frustration, and average daily performance. By recognizing the desire and motivation to work for yourself, the power of self-discipline will open the door to success.

THE INGREDIENTS OF SELF-DISCIPLINE

"A proper balance must be struck between indulgence and severity. However, severity, despite occasional mistakes, is preferable to a lack of discipline."
-I Ching (1150 B.C)

Self-discipline is a very powerful tool that can be developed for achieving about anything which you can dream. However, there are four key ingredients that must be present in our lives to allow self-discipline to flourish and exist. Most people have some or all of these key ingredients, but lack the knowledge of where and how to use them. Here are the four key ingredients of self-discipline:

1.　**Self-Control** – The act of controlling our emotions, actions, thoughts, words, and personal direction.

2. **Motivation** – The "fire inside", that fuels our efforts and makes accomplishments worth achieving.

3. **Persistence** – The ability to continue through adversity. The ability to brush off failure and stay focused on our goals.

4. **Goals** – Those tangible achievements that breed motivation and form our definitions of happiness and success.

All four of these ingredients must be present in our lives to achieve self-discipline. Every one of us knows a highly motivated person or two that just can't seem to do anything right. A friend or neighbor who has the goal of becoming self-employed, but just can't muster enough courage to take the first step. At one time or another, all of us have been motivated to do something, only to give up after the first failure. How many people go on a diet each year and gain more weight than they originally started with? How often have you created a household budget for you and your family, only to find yourself deeper in debt? These are examples of living without self-discipline. The reason we get depressed and frustrated when we pinch the fat on our midsection or thighs, is not because we lack a proper genetic make-up, but because we have undertaken a task without developing self-discipline.

In order to ensure our success at every endeavor, we must first understand how to strengthen and enhance each of the four key-ingredients needed for self-discipline. By understanding and practicing simple techniques that strengthen each ingredient, we open the door to success by eliminating our self-destructive behaviors. Once we become accustomed to recognizing and implementing these four ingredients, the programmed habit of self-discipline allows us to take control of our lives. Let's begin by examining each key-ingredient and learning simple techniques for enhancing their influence.

SELF-CONTROL

"I count him braver who overcomes his desires than him who conquers his enemies; for the hardest victory is over self."
-Aristotle (384 – 322 B.C.)

Learn to say NO to your destructive feelings, uncontrolled cravings, and selfish desires. Our primal and self-satisfying desires constantly demand appropriate control, and if we continue to satisfy the need of urges, we weaken our self-control. The narcotic of having everything all the time can dominate every action of our lives. When we begin to discriminate between what is actually needed and what is truly unnecessary, we develop a powerful sense of personal management.

The ability to control our emotions, actions, words, and thoughts has always been one of man's most difficult tasks. In today's society, we have made even the most outrageous overindulgence accessible by the simple push of a button. It is far more difficult to exert self-control over our lives today, than any other time in human history, and it shows!

Once we stop succumbing to every whim, craving, and desire we have, our self-control begins to strengthen and create a chain reaction. We become more alert and vigilant towards managing that which is good, and that which is unnecessary or bad. The power of self-control becomes strong enough to regulate our mental and physical cravings, society-induced desires, and influenced behaviors.

Once we have awakened self-control through the management of urges, we must reinforce it by creating the habit of denying ourselves that which we crave. Self-control acts as a filter against the powerful influence of advertising, accessibility, and our own destructive human habits. We live in a society where it is hard NOT to be fat, lazy, unhealthy, drugged up, bankrupt, depressed, or emotionally unstable. We have created so many conveniences, trends, wants, and erratic behaviors through advertising and mass media, that we are brainwashed to crave things.

The first step to gaining self-control is one of identifying the areas in our lives that are out of control. We have to take a close look at the food we eat, the bad habits we have, the character traits we possess, and the overall direction of our lives. Once we identify those things we need more control over, we can start small by gaining little victories each day. You must begin denying yourself one cigarette a day, the extra snack, that extra beer after work, or the satisfaction of indulging your emotional outbursts. If you try to go "cold-turkey" on all of your cravings, habits, and behaviors, you will surely fail.

A technique for gaining self-control over our cravings and habits involves a self-inspection of our daily lives. By performing an inventory of our bad behaviors and habits, we can focus our efforts on controlling them.

Here is a step by step description of this self-control technique:

1. **Personal Inventory** – Find a quiet and private place to sit down with a paper and pen. Begin taking a day by day inventory of your bad habits and destructive cravings.

2. **Start Small** – Begin reducing each habit or craving a little each day. Keep a journal of your progress and talk to yourself about the benefits of eliminating destructive behaviors.

3. **Self-Denial** – Start by denying yourself a certain pleasure each day. Target a daily activity like excessive eating or watching television.

4. **Keep a Schedule** – Make a to-do list and stick to it for a change. Make a commitment to write a daily schedule and accomplish every task.

5. **Review** – At the end of each day, sit down and critique your performance. Mentally re-live how you exercised self-control over your cravings and habits.

Another very effective technique is called the power band. This method involves wearing a piece of colored string or rubber band around your wrist to constantly remind yourself of the habit or craving you are going to control today. Take a large rubber band and write the bad habit or behavior that you wish to focus on for this particular day, and wear it around your wrist to constantly remind you of your control. I have personally seen this method change the lives of many people. Visualize in your mind that this rubber band empowers you with self-control that flows through your whole body. Every time you are faced with a certain thought, action, or environment that stimulates this craving or bad behavior, look to the power band for help. Remember that the power of your mind is the most important ally you have in the battle for self-control.

MOTIVATION

"Rest not! Life is sweeping by; go and do before you die.
Something mighty and sublime, leave behind to conquer time."
-Johann Goethe (1749 – 1832)

Motivation is the fuel that gives our success engine its drive. Motivation is a group of reasons that develop a desire to accomplish, have, act, and perform in a manner that will satisfy a certain desire. Strong motivation is the underlying power behind some of the world's greatest achievements. Motivation is responsible for creating actions, thoughts, and situations that are directed toward a specific accomplishment. There is no use in trying to master self-discipline if you lack the motivation to have it. Every human being has been motivated by some-thing at some point in their lives. The fact that you are reading this book shows that you have a certain degree of motivation to succeed at something.

The problem that most people encounter when trying to motivate themselves to achieve a certain goal, is the problem of false motivators. False motivation is the main problem behind most humans' poor daily performance. For example, the person who wakes up each and every day to go to work because he has to, and not because he wants to, is falsely motivated. The person that goes on a diet because his or her spouse wants them to is falsely motivated. The employee, who is told to perform a certain task because their boss told them to, is falsely motivated. These are all examples of why people perform poorly or experience lackluster results. True motivation is the result of a strong personal desire that focuses a person's thoughts, words, and actions in such a way as to elicit 100 percent effort. Imagine if you could muster the same motivation for performing at work, as you do for personal gain. How strong would your motivation be if you were promised one million dollars for showing up to work everyday this week?

The reason that Super-Humans live a life of greatness and success is because they are truly motivated to accomplish their goals. How many people achieve a life of greatness or success in a job that they hate? How financially disciplined is a person who works simply to pay off daily bills and not for the attainment of goals? How many A's did you receive in classes that you were completely uninterested in? When we stop and think about our daily lives, we can easily distinguish false and true motivators simply by looking at our performance in certain areas.

When you truly desire to control certain habits, cravings, and behaviors in your life, you already have one of the key ingredients to self-discipline. Most people know that they want control over certain aspects of their lives, but lack the motivation to bring about true change. One of the easiest methods for strengthening motivation is through pressure. By telling your family, friends, and co-workers of your commitment to control an aspect of your life, you establish the presence of external pressure. Now, the motivation for achieving discipline is embarrassment, self-esteem, and challenge. Peer pressure is a very powerful motivator for most people. Tell your family and friends of the commitment you have made to losing weight and exercising. Tell all of your co-workers of your personal challenge, and let everyone at lunch and dinner know of your low-fat diet and see how strong your motivation becomes.

Only through self-discipline can we begin to control and shape the direction of our lives, and only through proper motivation can we experience self-discipline. Always be aware of your level of motivation. Use different techniques and situations to strengthen your motivation in specific areas. Only by focusing on self-control and motivation first, can you expect to open the doors to a life of self-discipline.

PERSISTENCE

"Endurance is one of the most difficult disciplines, but it is to the one who endures that the final victory comes."
-Buddha (568 – 488 BC)

Persistence is the act of continued action and effort towards an objective, even in the face of multiple failures. Remember a time in your life when you kept after something again and again until you finally succeeded? How powerful and glorious did it feel to finally achieve your intended goal? How often in your daily life do you accept failure or the answer NO? Of all the bad habits, cravings, and behaviors which now exist in your life, how many times did you give up after failing to control them?

Self-discipline does not come without experiencing failure, and the only way to defeat failure is through persistence and perseverance. All of the world's past and present Super-Humans have found success and happiness with a never-say-die attitude. One of our country's most successful Super-Humans was also one of history's most persistent failures. Here is his story:

Abraham Lincoln

1831	Failed in business - declared bankruptcy.
1832	Defeated for State Legislature.
1834	Again failed in business – declares bankruptcy.
1835	Fiancée dies.
1836	Has a nervous breakdown.
1837	Defeated in election.
1843	Defeated in bid for U.S. Congress.
1846	Again defeated for U.S. Congress.
1847	Fails for a third time in bid for U.S. Congress.
1855	Defeated for U.S. Senate.
1856	Defeated for office of Vice President.
1858	Again defeated for U.S. Senate.
1859	Elected President of the United States of America.

The history books are full of Super-Humans who used the power of persistence to gain control of their destinies. The great Prime Minister of Great Britain, Winston Churchill, once said, "Success is going from failure to failure without a loss of enthusiasm." This is the most common reason for people's lack of self-discipline. It is because they failed once or twice at controlling their life that they become afraid to try again. Well, here is your chance to begin anew. By using the information and techniques found in this chapter, you will become better educated at how to achieve total control of your life. There is no magic formula or ancient Hindu technique for becoming persistent. All the perseverance and persistence you will ever need is deep inside you, waiting to be exercised.

Of the four ingredients required for self-discipline, persistence is probably the most powerful of the four, because without persistence you will never experience success. You must plan to never give up, even before you begin. If you mentally motivate yourself to keep trying no matter what, you will subconsciously program yourself for persistence. If you are motivated, have self-control, and set specific goals to achieve self-discipline, but give up at the first sign of failure, you will never experience self-discipline or success.

Persistence is the one ingredient that must always be present in order to succeed. Begin today by declaring your tenacity and vowing to never give up, no matter how long it takes. Make a point of going that extra mile. Learn to break out of your comfort zone and start testing the boundaries of your physical and mental limitations.

GOALS

"One should act in consonance with the way of Heaven and Earth, enduring and eternal, the superior man perseveres long in his course, adapts to the times, but remains firm in his direction and correct in his goals."
-I Ching (1150 BC)

Highly successful people, world leaders, great artists, and history's most important Super-Humans all have one thing in common: they use self-discipline on a daily basis to achieve their goals. Clear and specific goals are the essential foundation of not only self-discipline, but also a lifetime of health, wealth, and longevity. Without clearly defining short-term and lifelong goals, you have no use for self-discipline. Learning life mastery and personal discipline will only come about when you set precise goals that you wish to achieve. Self-discipline goals are somewhat different than success-oriented goals, in that self-discipline goals are defined by personal improvement. Once you identify areas of your life that you wish to gain total control over, you have now defined specific areas of improvement.

Self-discipline-oriented goals are essential to generating self-control, motivation, and persistence, the other three key ingredients needed for self-discipline. Here is an example of self-discipline goals:

1. I want to have total control over when, how, and what I eat for the next 30 days.

2. I am going to gain control of my finances by sticking to my scheduled budget each and every day for the next 90 days.

3. I want my fellow co-workers to look up to me as a leader and example of discipline by the way I speak, act, and dress in 60 days.

4. I will gain control of my emotions by disciplining my anger, depression, and attitude around my family, friends, and co-workers.

5. I am going to set aside one hour every day to work on my goal of being self-employed in one year.

6. I will set aside one hour each day to organizing, maintaining, and cleaning my household, my clothing, and my possessions.

7. I want to dedicate one evening each week to my spouse, and use this evening to improve our relationship and show my love and appreciation.

8. I will set a disciplined example for my children by becoming more involved in their lives, and showing them how I have gained control over my life.

9. I will discipline my body to quit smoking by gradually reducing the amount of cigarettes I smoke each week, until I have completely quit in 30 days.

10. I want to reduce the amount of television I watch to 45 minutes per day, by disciplining myself to use this time for constructive efforts.

As you can see from this list of self-discipline goals, the key to having discipline is to clearly define that for which you want to use it. By setting specific goals, you enact powerful mental forces that help you focus your thoughts, actions, and efforts to accomplishing them. Take the time to think about your personal improvement desires and clearly write them down. Make photocopies of your self-discipline goals, paste them all over your office, put them in your car, stick them to your bathroom mirror, and visualize yourself achieving total control. It is one thing to say that you want to lose weight, but it is another to clearly define the amount, how, and when you are going to lose the weight.

You must understand that simply wanting something is not enough, you must define, refine, focus, and schedule specific actions that you will take to have what you desire. The amazing power of self-discipline can alter your life to that of a Super-Human, by simply understanding the process and forces at work in the human body and mind. Remember that the four key-ingredients are specific guidelines by which you will ensure the greatest chance of success in your quest for self-discipline. Use the powerful techniques that you have learned in this chapter to prepare a personal battle plan for achieving your desires, wants, and goals.

Self-discipline can surely set you free and change your whole life, but you must pay attention to the four key-ingredients to insure total success. Tomorrow when you go to work, stop and look around at all of the people you see, and think about how a self-disciplined person would act, talk, and look. Use the power of self-discipline to enhance your wealth, happiness, and the lives of your loved ones. Make the commitment to gain total control of your life today, and you will thank yourself tomorrow. Know that it is possible to rise above average human performance, by dedicating time each day to achieve the status of a disciplined human.

GENERATIONAL DISCIPLINE

"In every one of us there are two ruling and directing principles, whose guidance we follow wherever they may lead; the one being an innate desire of pleasure; the other, an acquired judgment which aspires after excellence."
--Socrates (469-399 B.C.)

In today's fast-paced world of technology, stress, and two-job households, life can seem like a ride on a burning Ferris wheel. Sometimes we can become so caught up in the schedule of everyday life that we fail to notice the impression we leave behind. If you stop and think about it, everything we do and say leaves an impression on the people around us. Whether it's our co-workers, family, or friends with whom we interact, our commitment to personal discipline is the foundation of our perceived character.

Although we might not realize it, each day we leave an indelible impression of our personal self-worth, beliefs, work ethic, and character with every person with whom we come in contact. Over a period of days, weeks, and years these little impressions begin to build a picture or "advertisement" of our character for others to see. It is human nature to make mistakes, but it is also human nature to overlook the legacy of daily impressions we leave behind.

Generational discipline is the legacy that each of us leaves behind for our friends, spouses, and children to remember us by. It is also the legacy of our work ethic that our co-workers, employers, and customers remember us by. Each day that we show up to work, interact, and perform a task, we are building our own "advertisement" for others to see. The little things that we do might not seem like a big deal at the time, but over the course of our lifetime, they amount to nothing less than our character image. Words like reliable, selfless, exuding commitment and integrity describe a person that cares about his or her daily performance.

Have you ever thought about how your actions affect the lives of your children, spouse, and family? As an example of generational discipline, let's take a look at the lives of two men: Max Jukes and Jonathan Edwards. Max Jukes was an Atheist who believed in the abolition of laws and rules. Mr. Jukes believed in and preached about a lifestyle of free sex, no laws, no formal education and no responsibilities. Jonathan Edwards was known by all as the "disciplinarian". Not because he disciplined his children harshly, but because he was a self-disciplined man. He became a preacher that believed in leading by example. He authored two books on the subjects of responsibility and integrity. Mr. Edwards became known for teaching people from all walks of life how to be responsible for their actions. Both of these men came from very similar backgrounds, but developed opposing lifestyles and beliefs. The only common ground these men shared, was that they both fathered 13 children. Here are the legacies they left behind:

MAX JUKES	**JONATHON EDWARDS**
1026 descendants	929 descendants
LEGACY	**LEGACY**
300 convicts	430 ministers
190 prostitutes	86 college professors
536 alcoholics and drug addicts	75 authors
	13 university presidents
	7 Congressman
	3 Governors
	1 Vice-President of the United States

There is no question that developing self-discipline will change your life for the better, but real results can only be seen in the legacy of performance we leave behind. When we begin to use self-discipline to control our emotional highs and lows, our appearance, our work ethic, and our commitment to physical exercise, we are doing much more than improving our own lives. Our ability to begin focusing on our daily performance is directly proportional to the success our generations will experience. Remember that personal achievement is not only about you, your job, your bank account, or even your own personal satisfaction. Developing self-discipline for a lifetime of above-average performance and prosperity is about the legacy you leave behind.

Take time to slow down and examine your actions, words, and thoughts throughout the day. Make it a priority to develop the trait of self-discipline. Begin to focus on the "advertisement" that you display to your co-workers, friends, and family. The ability to control your life through the power of self-discipline is not only the secret to a lifetime of success, but the deciding factor in the legacy you leave behind- a legacy of self-discipline.

MISSION #1

"There are countless ways of achieving greatness, but any road to achieving one's maximum potential must be built on a bedrock of respect for the individual, a commitment to excellence, and a rejection of mediocrity."
-Buck Rogers

To successfully accomplish the first mission, I need you to take your time in thinking about each question that you are asked. I want you to use a pencil and notebook to answer these questions. I urge you to keep a personal journal of all the information you will gather from reading this book. Once you are satisfied that you have answered honestly, thoughtfully, and without external motivators, you can move on to the next chapter. For this mission I don't want you to talk with your spouse or friends about the questions, and I don't want you to talk to anyone about the results.

This is a personal mission that only you can accomplish. Once you have answered all of the questions in your notebook, I want you to sit down and take a look at your life from this perspective. This mission is based upon a technique we use in the SEAL Teams to discipline ourselves by taking a serious, yet objective look at our strengths and weaknesses.

1. ARE YOU OVERWEIGHT?
2. WHAT IS YOUR AGE?
3. HOW MUCH DO YOU WEIGH?
4. HOW TALL ARE YOU?
5. RATE THE STRESS YOUR JOB PUTS ON YOU? FROM 1-10.
6. HOW MANY HOURS PER WEEK DO YOU WORK?
7. HOW MUCH MONEY PER MONTH WOULD MAKE YOU HAPPY AND SUCCESSFUL?
8. WHAT IS YOUR DREAM HOME LIKE AND WHERE WOULD YOU LIVE?
9. HOW OFTEN DO YOU WORK ON YOUR FUTURE GOALS?
10. HOW MANY MINUTES OR HOURS DO YOU EXERCISE PER WEEK?
11. DO YOU SMOKE? HOW MANY CIGARETTES PER WEEK?
12. HOW MANY BEERS OR DRINKS DO YOU CONSUME PER WEEK?
13. WHAT IS YOUR FAVORITE HOBBY?

14. WHAT ILLNESS, DISORDER, OR CHRONIC PAIN DO YOU HAVE?
15. HOW MANY TIMES DO YOU EAT RED MEAT PER WEEK?
16. HOW WOULD YOU RANK YOUR DIET? FROM 1-10?
17. DO YOU EAT AT LEAST 3 SERVINGS OF FRUITS AND VEGETABLES PER DAY?
18. HOW MUCH PERSONAL QUIET TIME DO YOU HAVE PER DAY?
19. ARE YOUR HOUSE, POSSESSIONS, PAPERWORK, OFFICE, VEHICLES, AND FINANCES WELL ORGANIZED?
20. HOW WOULD YOU RANK YOUR MARRIAGE OR RELATIONSHIP? FROM 1-10?
22. HOW WOULD YOU RANK YOUR ABILITY TO FOLLOW A SET BUDGET? FROM 1-10?
23. ARE YOU HAPPY WITH YOUR BODY?
24. HOW MUCH SLEEP DO YOU AVERAGE PER DAY?
25. HOW MANY HOURS PER WEEK DO YOU WATCH TV?

MISSION DE-BRIEF

"What it lies in our power to do, it lies in our power not to do."
Aristotle

In the SEAL Teams we dissect, discuss, and write down everything about our training and real world missions. We will sit around for hours, going over and over every little mistake, detail, and occurrence that transpired from the very beginning to the very end of our mission. I have been in de-briefs that have lasted over five hours for just a simple jungle patrol. You can imagine how much scrutiny every move you make comes under. As a Navy SEAL Sniper, I was taught the value of knowing all you can about your enemy through intelligence gathering. I also learned that in order to accomplish a specific task or mission, you must know exactly what your assets, capabilities, and weaknesses are.

One of the most important skills I have learned as a SEAL, is to always write down everything you have learned, accomplished, or failed at, in a journal. This journal is carried with us everywhere we go, and is like a computer hard drive that stores all of the information that goes into being a Navy SEAL. We call this journal our "BAG OF TRICKS" because it has all of the little tidbits, ideas, tools, and information that we individually learn to make us more knowledgeable and effective.

The information you now have from accomplishing Mission #1 must be de-briefed just like any operation or mission. You must keep this information as a beginning to your bag of tricks, and use it to improve your effectiveness and knowledge in the battle to master self-discipline. I strongly encourage you to find a quiet place to sit down. Begin thinking about what this information means to you, and how you can use it to organize yourself to become more efficient and self-disciplined.

CHAPTER 2 – THE BATTLE OF THE BRAIN

"No horse gets anywhere until he is harnessed. No stream or gas drives anything until it is confined. No Niagara is ever turned into light and power until it is tunneled. No life ever grows great until it is focused, dedicated, disciplined."

-Harry Emerson Fosdick

The human brain is the most glorious and deadly weapon put upon this great planet. The power of the mind is like nuclear energy; if harnessed properly it can provide unlimited power for good, but if it is misused and then allowed to randomly radiate through your body and life, it can slowly cause your death. In the SEAL Teams we spend about five times as much effort training our mental focus as we do training our bodies. With the dawning of the digital age we can now find as many pleasure devices for the mind as we can for the body. There is so much input of useful and useless information today, that it is extremely hard to separate the two.

Today, we find ourselves having more mental habits than we do physical habits, and these mental habits destroy our bodies just as quickly as do our physical habits. Since I am by no means a psychiatrist or brain surgeon, I will steer clear of using million dollar words and professional jargon that serve only to confuse us even further. The human brain is much like your body, in that it requires proper and clean fuel, exercise, stimulation, and rest in order to function at optimal levels. The brain or computer you carry in your head is just as unique to you as your body, and can be sculpted, strengthened, and enhanced in a similar fashion. However, it can be slowly poisoned, neglected, malnourished, and misunderstood to the point that it begins to break down and ultimately die.

In this chapter I will give you examples of techniques we use in the special operations world to harness and cultivate the power of the mind, along with a few tricks to help you focus your concentration and bring the power of self-discipline to your mind. Before we get too far ahead into techniques of reprogramming your computer, we must first identify a few common glitches and their effects upon our lives.

The list of glitches and consequences is not meant to insult your intelligence, and is of course by no means a complete or all-inclusive list. It is however a reminder of the effects and consequences we must eventually face when we have no defense or system of eliminating them from our minds and life. Mental discipline is not something you can buy or borrow, it is inside all of us from the time we are born. It is through the process of living that we put it on a shelf and forget its impact, but by dusting it off and reprogramming our minds to use it once again, we are able to formulate a set of mental guidelines.

DISCIPLINE DEFICIENCY

GLITCH	CONSEQUENCE
Overeating	Fat, unhealthy body and finally death
Smoking	Lung cancer, arterial sclerosis, and death
Drinking	Addiction, liver disease, and death
Uncleanness	Appearance, disease, no self confidence, and death
Anything goes diet	Weak brain, fat body, disease, sickness, and death
Procrastination	Loss of job, family, possessions, and reputation
Anger	Loss of freedom, job, family, bodily harm, and death
Depression	Disease, misery, loss of confidence, and death
Poor appearance	Loss of job, respect, reputation, confidence, and love
Stress	Heart attack, disease, loss of family, job, and death
Obsession	Financial ruin, addiction, loss of family, job, death
Selfishness	Loss of family, friends, reputation, peace, selfworth
Greed	Loss of job, family, friends, financial ruin, and death
No exercise	Fat, unhealthy body & mind, disease, and death
Cravings	Fat, unhealthy body & mind, loss of family, death
Complacency	Loss of job, family, possessions, respect, love
Laziness	Loss of job, friends, family, possessions, productivity
Lack of discipline	**see all of above!**

It is human nature to seek out pleasure and comfort in life, but we are weakened when we overindulge and lose our ability to control moderation. I will never profess to having mastered the power of self-discipline, but I know and see the results of applying it to not only the elite world of special operations, but to everyday life. Our brains, although extremely complex, operate in a very logical and simple manner. I would like you to picture your brain as a beautiful painting, and think of self-discipline as the artist. The artist has thousands of colors from which to choose and many different brushes with which to apply them. Without an artist to control and apply the exact amount and placement of color, we end up with a confusing mirage that has no order. When we use the artist (self-discipline) to control all aspects of the painting, we end up with a beautiful work of art.

In the SEAL Teams we use self-discipline to control or diminish the effects of pain, fear, sorrow, complacency, selfishness, and anger to help provide clarity during moments of intense physical and mental overload. The term overload applies to the condition when external physical or mental experiences shock the body and mind into a state of single-mindedness. Have you ever been in such great pain or extreme anger that you could not control your reaction? How about when you smashed your thumb with a hammer, or slammed a door on your fingers? Your mind experienced such overload that you probably yelled obscenities, jumped up and down, cried, and basically your body did things you weren't telling it to do.

This same phenomenon can be used to control your body when you do experience mental or physical overload. We call this technique "muscle memory" because we are actually exercising a programmed response to occur when a certain type of overload shocks our brain.

The subconscious mind is being used when you perform tasks about which you really don't remember thinking. Like when you get in your car after a long and hard day of work and the next thing you know you are sitting in your driveway wondering how you got there. This is the phenomenon known as the subconscious mind. This "second mind" is able to perform tasks twice as fast as the conscious mind, because it is pre-programmed to perform a certain task without conscious thought.

It is a known fact, that the fastest you can draw a pistol from your holster while thinking through the whole process is around 1.5 seconds, but with a pre-programmed muscle memory reaction of drawing your pistol, this can be accomplished in around .3 to .6 seconds. This same reprogramming technique can be found in most professional sports today. In order for a basketball player to dribble the basketball with both hands while running and thinking about the tactics of the game, he must have muscle memory to dribble the basketball.

Imagine being a batter up at the plate in a professional baseball game. You must not only be thinking of the tactical situation of the runners on base, but the number of strikes and balls you have, the speed of the ball, the location and spin of the ball, and finally time your swing to intersect a 95mph sphere. Obviously there are too many things happening at once to consciously think about them all and intercept the ball with the bat at the precise moment.

In order for a person to be successful at this endeavor, certain tasks must be committed to the subconscious mind by the technique of muscle memory. The trained response of swinging the bat occurs when a certain event triggers it, such as your eye seeing the ball in a certain location at a certain time. In most people, the ability to retain a certain muscle memory function usually occurs after 3,000 to 3,200 repetitions of a certain action. However, some smaller tasks only require 100 to 500 repetitions, like tying a new knot or typing on a keyboard.

REPROGRAMMING THE COMPUTER

"Taking time is a thief's trade, making time a strategist's. An effective manager must be both a strategist and thief, stealing time from less compelling or more leisurely pursuits to get the job done."
-Lewis Kelly

In each of our brains, we have three totally separate and distinct entities. Many different doctors, self-professed experts, and psychiatrists call these three entities many different things. In the SEAL Teams we commonly call these three different entities the conscious mind, the subconscious mind, and the mind's eye. Previously, I talked a little about the conscious and subconscious minds, and about how they operate. However, in order to become a seeker and practitioner of self-discipline, we must form a working knowledge and basic understanding of how our computer works.

Below I have broken down these three distinct entities of the brain into a simple definition-explanation format. Keep in mind, there is a limitless amount of information and ideas out there for you to study and dissect about the workings of the brain. For the seeker of self-discipline, the attainment of knowledge is like the weapons you see the action-adventure heroes carrying in the movies. It never runs out of ammunition and is always there to defeat his enemies. By always seeking to learn more about how, where, and why our brains function, we are in a sense giving ourselves an endless supply of ammunition to combat our mental enemies.

The conscious mind

This part of the brain has as its main function the survival of the body; it wants you to preserve your life. It files experiences of pain and pleasure, but its method of information input is through the five main physical senses. The five main physical senses are: touch, taste, sound, sight, and smell. The conscious mind is an extension of the human physical necessities. It is the guide in our struggles for the material environment, and its highest function is that of reasoning.

The subconscious mind

This part of the brain has as its main function the storage and acquisition of information. It is where your mind's eye and conscious mind go for answers or input. The subconscious mind has memory, and all of our thoughts, actions, and experiences are stored there in perfect condition. Many reactions we experience as adults come from distant childhood memories. The subconscious mind responds to suggestion and programming much like a computer. Through self-discipline, meditation, suggestion, and muscle-memory, we can control our thoughts and thus control and use the subconscious mind for peace, enhanced performance, organization, happiness, and instant action. The subconscious mind takes its input independently of the five physical senses. It perceives intuition and is the seat of emotion, memory, and the storeroom of information. It performs its highest function when the conscious mind has relinquished control.

The mind's eye

This is the third and most underestimated entity of the brain. The mind's eye is the picture, movie, or video screen that is present in our thoughts. The mind's eye is the television we use in our brain to view all of the images we formulate from the past, present, and desired future. When we close our eyes and view certain images that we induce through thought, we are using the mind's eye. This eye is much more powerful than the two we have sitting beside our nose. It possesses the ability to elicit pain, pleasure, power, riches, happiness, sadness, just about every emotion we can feel or express. The other two eyes have only the ability to give input at an exact moment and time. The mind's eye is the main programming tool of the subconscious mind and can alter moods, feelings, thoughts, and actions by means of internal visual stimulation.

POWER LIVING IS YOUR MASTERPIECE

"Is there not a certain satisfaction, in the fact that natural limits are set to the life of the individual, so that at its conclusion it may appear as a work of art?"
-Albert Einstein

These words are extremely pertinent coming from Einstein, for when he died at the age of seventy-five, he left his greatest work unfinished. Yet Einstein died a very content and satisfied man, for he immensely enjoyed each moment of his life spent in pursuit of scientific excellence. This is the priceless lesson that seems to elude most humans. The goal to living a life of success, achievement, happiness, and health is not always about the end result, but rather the quality of the journey that we take in pursuit of our goals. The principle reason for a person's failure in his quest for success is a lack of confidence and too much misguided effort.

Many people block the door to success by failing to fully comprehend the workings of their subconscious mind. When you know how your success mechanism works, you gain the powerful weapon of self-confidence. You must remember that when your subconscious mind accepts an idea, it immediately begins to execute it. It uses all of its mighty resources to that end and mobilizes all of the mental and spiritual laws of your deeper mind. This law holds true for both good and bad ideas. Consequently, if you flood your mind with negative thoughts and statements, it brings trouble, failure, and confusion. When you begin thinking like a super-human bent on enhancing your present performance in life, it brings guidance, freedom, and peace of mind. The right answer and proper action are inevitable when your thoughts are positive, constructive, and loving. From this, it is perfectly clear that the one thing you must do to overcome failure is to accept the super-human idea that you control your destiny. Let your subconscious mind begin feeling its reality now, and the law of your mind will do the rest.

A car owner once argued with a mechanic for charging three hundred dollars for fixing his engine. The mechanic said, "I charged ten cents for the missing bolt and two hundred ninety-nine dollars and ninety-five cents for knowing how to fix what was wrong with your car. "Think of your mind as the master mechanic, the all-knowing one, who knows ways and means of healing any organ of your body, as well as generating the answers for your success. Decree success, and your mind will establish it, but clarity and relaxation are the keys. Do not be so concerned with the details and daily struggles, but know the ultimate end result. Get the feel of the happy solution to your problems whether it is financial, health, love, or work. Remember how you felt after you accomplished something significant. Keep in mind that this feeling is the cornerstone of all subconscious reactions. Your new lease on life must be felt subjectively in a finished, powerful, beautiful, and tranquil state, not in the future, but as coming about now.

By enacting and understanding, and not only reading, you will have the opportunity to be a true master of your own performance and destiny. You can make your world exactly what you want it to be, the decision is yours. If you want this incredible power and existence, the secret is to remember that your mind is the master mechanic of your performance and success. If you are able to design and regulate your thoughts, you master your mind and actions. Once you master your mind and actions, you begin the transformation to Power Living.

Pain is the ultimate teacher of lessons. Begin taking responsibility for your life and all of the circumstances and events that are in it. If you are unhappy, wish for more money, a better job, decide to make the changes and take positive action to elevate your performance and grasp your destiny. If you desire a sexier, healthier, and more energized body, take the steps necessary to achieve greater results and benefits. If you want a more loving and caring relationship, make the commitment to becoming the kind of person that attracts and nurtures such a life. None of this will come to you by chance, genetics, or inactivity; if you continue to perform at your present level, nothing will change and your present life will continue to be reality.

A masterpiece is a work of art or symbol of enduring talent, beauty, and revered greatness to be admired by all human beings. Each and every one of us has a blank canvas on which to create our own living and breathing masterpiece. The one consistent value that we all must recognize in the journey to achieving our destiny is pure and simple change. What empowers each of us with the ability to make decisions that change our lives is the ability to take consistent action. The power to control the outcome of our lives is directly related to the amount of control we have over our consistent actions and decisions. The golden rule to controlling change in our lives is: take action, any action, as long as we are constantly acting and moving in the direction of our wants and desires, we exert tremendous power towards the attainment of our desired reality.

THE 3 SECRETS OF MASTERING CHANGE

1. *Know and see your goals.*
2. *Modify and try, try, and try again, until you get the desired result.*
3. *Take action, any action will do.*

MUSCLE MEMORY

"Procrastination is like being a mosquito in a nudist camp, you know what you want to do, but you just don't know where to begin"
-SEAL Team saying

Muscle memory is the process of training our subconscious mind to accomplish certain thoughts and actions, through the mental or physical use of repetition. Just as we use repetition to condition ourselves to perform a certain physical task, we can likewise use muscle memory to perform a mental task without conscious thought. For example, if every time we saw a piece of chocolate cake we began to crave and hunger for it, we have a pre-programmed response to chocolate cake. If we refocus our mind's eye to view pictures of chocolate cake with maggots crawling all over it, and by viewing these images over and over in our mind's eye, we begin building a muscle memory response to chocolate cake. This muscle memory response will subconsciously bring up these disgusting images and associated feelings the next time we come across a piece of chocolate cake. What we have begun to do is replace the thoughts of craving and hunger, with repulsion and fullness.

Another application for muscle memory exists in the power of words. If hearing the word "work", elicits feelings and thoughts of failure, tedious labor, stress, and anxiety, we are acting out a pre-programmed muscle memory response. Conversely, if we conjure up images, thoughts, and feelings of joy, success, fun, and money, then associate these over and over again with the word "work" in our mind, we will have reprogrammed our muscle memory. The good news is that we don't need nearly as much practice or repetition for mental association as we do for physical skills. The bad news is that if we fail to practice these mental association skills, we will gradually revert back to the original negative feelings, thoughts, and emotions.

In order for us to create muscle memory for positive, productive, and pleasant reactions, we must first find out exactly what needs to be fixed. In Chapter #1 we took an inventory of our physical glitches and possessions to get the big picture of where we stand in life. At the end of this chapter you will go on another mission to find out who you are. The mission at the end of this chapter is designed to answer the question of exactly what needs to be fixed or reprogrammed in our minds. Once we have retrieved this information from our fact-finding mission, we can begin to use the techniques, tools, and information that you are now learning.

The technique of reprogramming the mind's eye is just a fancy word for visualization. Visualization is the active process of making a movie that we direct and watch over and over again in our mind's eye. The technique of visualization is one of the greatest reasons for the sheer success, precision, ferociousness, and control that the U.S. Navy SEAL Teams have experienced.

Every highly successful person who ever was, or ever will be, uses visualization. The human mind is extremely powerful, but as the owners of this great tool, we use only about 15% of it. I am sure all of you have heard the amazing stories of grandmothers lifting vehicles off of people, or the mental ability of some people to move objects and foresee events from the past and future. My intent is not to get sidetracked into subjects of the paranormal, but to simply re-affirm what you probably already know. If scientists, psychiatrists, doctors, and experts were correct in calculating the 15% total usage of the brain, then logic would dictate that we have the capacity to perform those amazing mental feats somewhere in the other 85% of our brains.

Pain is the most powerful and reaction-causing feeling that we can experience as humans. Pain is a physical and mental defense mechanism built into our bodies by nature to ensure survival. Mental pain can evoke just as many powerful reactions as physical pain, and often more easily. Just as physical pain can come from thousands of different actions or occurrences, mental pain can be experienced through words, actions, thoughts, and suggestions. Mental pain has a much more powerful and lasting effect on our lives than we can imagine. The death, destruction, and utter travesty that usually follow severe mental pain can be found everyday in your newspaper or on your television. The jealous husband, the slighted co-worker, an envious neighbor, or even the attention-starved school child is easily capable of committing atrocities in today's society when the ability to control mental pain is non-existent.

One day several years ago, I was restless and couldn't sleep very well. I decided to drive to the SEAL Team gym at around 1:30 in the morning. When I changed my clothes and walked towards the gym, I noticed a light on and some music playing over the sound system. Since it is a common occurrence to see other SEALs in the gym at any hour of the night, I didn't give it a second thought. I walked very quickly to the door of the gym, due to the fact that it was early February and very cold outside, when I noticed a soft thumping sound coming from around the backside of the building. The thumping sounds began to grow louder and I noticed a soft, oriental style of music as I walked closer to the rear of the building. When I turned the corner, I saw a fellow SEAL and friend of mine by the name of "Goat", who was kneeling on the cold pavement without any clothes on. Goat was rhythmically striking a *makawara* board – a thick wooden post bolted to the pavement and covered with rice straw by thin ropes.

His concentration was so complete that he was unaware of my presence. Blood was trickling from Goat's knuckles onto the board, but he kept smashing it smoothly and powerfully over and over for several minutes before looking up. He then rose to greet me. I reached out and shook his powerful hand, and again noticed the blood trickling off of his knuckles. I looked at his raw meat-like hand and asked him if that hurt very much. Goat said that he had not felt the pain until just this moment when he thought about it. "That's really going to hurt in the morning Goat, you might want to stop beating the ____ out of yourself," I said. Goat just looked at me and grinned a strange smile and told me the following story.

"When I was in Vietnam, I befriended an old man that taught Tai-Chi to the local village children. When I wasn't out on SEAL operations, I would spend as much time with him as I could. One day I came back from several days of chasing down V.C in the jungle and went to visit the old man, only to find him walking around with a large bandage around his stomach. He proceeded to tell me that he had been accidentally stabbed with a bamboo stick, and that it had become severely infected. He told me that in the morning he was going to the army medical tent to let the American doctors cut it out, and asked if I would accompany him to help translate.

"I agreed and met him the following morning at the Army's medical tent. The doctors told me that he would have to be operated on, and then tried to give him an anesthetic to put him out. When he immediately refused, the doctors told me that if he did not accept the anesthetic, they could not perform the operation, but the old man was insistent. After some discussion, the doctors finally agreed and asked me to help hold him down. The old man asked to be given a couple of minutes to prepare himself, and lay down on the table and closed his eyes. When he opened them, he said that it was O.K to begin and that it was unnecessary for me to hold him down.

"The doctors looked at each other in amazement and began to cut out this large infection from his stomach. The surgery lasted about an hour and a half, and the old man never moved, spoke, or flinched even once. When the surgery was over he got up quickly from the table and began to get dressed, and we all looked at each other in stunned amazement. As we were walking out of the tent I asked the old man how he had done such a feat. He replied that he was in fact not even there for the surgery, but in a very special place. Later, he taught me to focus my eyes and mind on a tiny spot on the ceiling or floor, and to regulate my breathing into a slow and steady rhythm.

"He told me that by focusing on that spot, he was able to take his mind away to a pleasant time and location he had created in his imagination. In this place he had a great banquet of food, and that he had concentrated on feeling, tasting, smelling, and enjoying the incredible tastes it had to offer. The pain that the doctors spoke of could not reach him if he was not present."

Goat later went on to tell me that he was just practicing the mental exercise of removing himself from his conscious mind, and was in the process of being physically adored by 12 beautiful women when I interrupted. Goat then looked around and said that if I didn't mind, could he teach me this later because he was now freezing his butt off and his knuckles hurt. I went on to sponge as much information and knowledge as I could from him, and continue to use and practice this simple and effective mental bodybuilding technique. This technique can be used for every mental emotion, feeling, and thought that is bad or harmful to our peace of mind and success. When we feel ourselves getting angry, depressed, or stressed out, we can use our mind's eye to create and view an interactive movie that takes us away to a pleasant and serene place.

The mind's eye can also provide a springboard for our financial and job-related success. By using this simple technique to visualize ourselves giving that perfect presentation, getting a promotion, or closing the big deal, we are in effect living our desired outcome before it even happens. Before I go on a mission or training exercise at work, I visualize in my mind's eye every step, word, action, and possible scenario that I will be asked to perform. This process helps me catch and eliminate any possible wrong move, thought, or reaction I may have, and by doing this over and over again I begin building up muscle memory for success.

The power of visualization is an extension of suggestion. Suggestion is the overall technique of applying visualization, muscle memory, thought repetition, and positive reprogramming skills to negative and mental glitches. By understanding and applying these techniques of suggestion, we are actually practicing the power of self-discipline. When you see the runner who is up bright and early everyday no matter what the weather, do you say to yourself "Wow, that person has a lot of self-discipline?" How about the co-worker that shows up early every day with a sharp, crisp, and well-groomed appearance to go along with his tireless energy and pleasant attitude? These are all examples of self-discipline manifesting itself in different ways, and I will bet that both of these people utilize some form of these techniques without even realizing it.

If we stop to think about it, there are situations every day where we can actually practice mental self-discipline. For example, I like to exercise and test my mental techniques of suggestion when I feel hunger. When I get that grumbling in my stomach, or thoughts of giant cheeseburgers and French fries play in my mind, I instinctively pause and recognize the mental and physical reactions that are occurring. Sometimes I will even go so far as to buy a cheeseburger and set it down in front of me, then experience the smell, visualize the taste, and let my mouth begin to salivate. I pick it up and throw it away or give it to someone else to eat. I then sit down to my pre-packed lunch, revel in my success, and treat my body right. Please don't get me wrong by thinking that self-discipline is the act of doing without, or of self-abuse, but rather the act of control and substitution. Instead of sleeping until 10:00 am and getting up to watch football, you merely substitute that schedule for one of getting up at 5:00 am and running before having a healthy breakfast. I hope that this is all getting through to you, and that you are now beginning to understand what is wrong with your computer and how to go about fixing it.

A series of thoughts or a statement can be called a belief. A belief is another word for our mental guidelines or personal set of rules. As we discussed in chapter #1, some of us follow our beliefs and some of us don't. Our beliefs are formed by us, and are guidelines for our words, actions, and behavior. Now that we have learned how to reprogram our thoughts, actions, and behaviors, we must now begin to identify and change our "destructive beliefs."

Our beliefs, or personal set of rules and regulations, frame the way we see reality, create reality, and live reality. As we have learned, beliefs reside in the subconscious mind and undermine the good intentions we hold at the conscious level. We must identify and change our negative beliefs that turn into glitches, bad habits, or destructive behaviors. Below I have listed several negative beliefs that always result in destructive thoughts and behavior.

DESTRUCTIVE MENTAL BELIEFS

BELIEF	*CONSEQUENCE*
"I just can't do it, it's too hard!"	You will never do it - ever.
"I am just too tired right now."	You will always be too tired.
"I don't like my body or appearance."	Nobody else will like them either.
"I am getting too old to do that."	You will die young and bored.
"I can't help myself, I just can't resist!	You will never help yourself.
"I am afraid to say what I feel."	You will have no real opinion.
"I will always be fat!"	You will always be fat.

The amazing powers of the human mind should never be underestimated. If you stop and listen to your inner voice from time to time, you will discover the answer to most of your problems. The answer lies in the negative statements we make to ourselves that bring about negative circumstances. The old adage of "you are what you think", is one of the basic laws of human nature. Take the time to investigate your own beliefs and thought patterns. Begin to eliminate the constant barrage of negative programming by focusing on positive thoughts of accomplishment. Use the power of discipline to program your mind for success and happiness.

THE SIXTH SENSE

"To enjoy good health, to bring true happiness to one's family, to bring peace to all, one must first discipline and control one's mind. If a man can control his mind he can find the way to enlightenment, and all wisdom and virtue will naturally come to him."
Buddha (568 – 488 B.C.)

There is a powerful secret that some of the world's most powerful and influential people keep closely guarded. This powerful human ability is beginning to be recognized as an important creative planning and problem-solving tool for today's super-human achiever. This powerful secret is called the sixth sense. Intuition is no longer seen as a special gift that is given to a select few. Intuition is the power that feeds, enhances, and ignites your focused visions or ideas. This misunderstood human ability enables the executive to foresee a clear solution during a time of need, change, or in the face of hard economic times. This amazing human ability known as a hunch, insight, gut feeling, or sudden inspiration, is the foundation of focused intuition. In the SEAL

Teams we call this our sixth sense, which can create correct solutions and decisions before all of the facts are known. Focused intuition is the generator of success.

You have probably never heard a world leader or top executive say in public, "I had a hunch and went with it" in order to make a crucial decision, hire a particular person, adopt a radical policy change, or take a risky gamble. Yet most of today's high achieving super-humans combine their sixth sense with logic to greatly enhance their decision-making ability in all aspects of life. Listen closely, and you may hear clues of a gut feeling, intuition, or a last-minute judgment call that lead to a certain high-powered decision. Today' super-human does not ignore facts, figures, and logic, but each uses focused intuition input to add weight, or solidify a certain course of action.

In the SEAL Teams we regard the sixth sense as a crucial part of every important decision. There are many instances in the world of special operations where a particular door, route, path, area, or situation just didn't feel right and the mission was either changed or cancelled. Surprisingly enough, most of these decisions proved to be absolutely correct. Several times throughout my career as a Navy SEAL, countless lives have been saved because of a hunch, strong feeling, or sixth sense.

The sixth sense is simply a way of characterizing the mind's subconscious ability to instantly draw stored information, ideas, and feelings from its memory banks and turn it into a suggestion or emotion. Intuition can come as a flash or as a flow of ideas and suggestions, each one effecting the next until you have a clear pattern of innovative thoughts and actions.

Throughout the course of your life, you have undoubtedly used intuition at some time or another to make a decision. Maybe it was at the car lot when you just felt "wrong" about a particular vehicle, or maybe when you met somebody for the fist time and felt something negative about them, or even decided not to take a certain street for some unknown reason. These are all example of intuition and your sixth sense providing input during the decision making process. Most people have heard the stories of people deciding not to get on a particular flight or take a certain bus because something inside their mind was telling them not to, only to find out the plane crashed or the bus went over a cliff. This same powerful ability can be exercised and harnessed to provide clarity and input to our everyday decisions.

Throughout my career in the special operations world, I had the pleasure of studying and interacting with many of the world's primitive cultures. All of these cultures use intuition as a major source of information and decision making. In South and Central America, the Indian tribes that live along the Amazon and deep in the jungles, believe that a spirit talks to them inside their head. This spirit offers advice, guidance, and often prophecies of things to come. The American Indians believe that the Great Spirit and ancestral spirits guide them with advice and solutions. The Eskimo's believe that certain animal spirits talk to them during times of duress or uncertainty with hints of advice and guidance.

Throughout time these cultures have used devices and drugs to help promote the sixth sense or "inner voice", by using sweat lodges, opium, peyote, and other trance inducing concoctions. I have spent considerable time with some tribes that use the sixth sense to determine the course of each day, whether it is hunting, fishing, working, celebrating, or spiritual reflection. Some days were judged to be good hunting days simply because it felt "right" or an inner voice told them so.

How can you keep in touch with your sixth sense and tap into the amazing power of intuition? Many Far East holy men, ancient culture spiritual leaders, high-powered corporate executives, and world leaders use a variety of techniques to exercise and harness the power of intuition on a regular basis. Here are seven powerful techniques and exercises that come from the jungles of South America, the boardrooms of high-powered executives, and the prayer rooms of Tibet. Try out and practice each one of these techniques to strengthen and harness your sixth sense. You might find some of these a little odd or awkward, just remember that the sixth sense cannot be quantified, but nearly everyone agrees it is there.

Intuition Games

Playing intuition games is a powerful technique for tapping into your sixth sense. Ask your co-workers or family members to guess who will come into the room next and what they will be wearing. Guess what your friends or family will say next when having a conversation. If you are going to meet somebody new, guess what clothes they will be wearing or their physical features from their personal facts, like age, race, and sex. When you are sitting beside someone in a plane or bus, try to visualize what this person does for a living first, and then ask him or her.

Brainstorming

Use the power of visualization to open up your sixth sense. Close your eyes and imagine a large white wall with the words "advantages" and "disadvantages" written in big black letters. Under the word "advantages", mentally list all of the positive ways to solve this particular problem. As you mentally write each possible solution, take a deep breath and visually see this solution in action from beginning to end. Go through the list of advantages for each solution and clearly focus on all possible outcomes of using this solution.

As you visualize these ideas, does one stand out more than others? Does this idea just "feel" right? Keep these ideas firmly planted in your image and now visualize the word "disadvantages". Mentally write all of the possible factors that could produce an undesired outcome from each of the ideas. By concentrating the brain's power of imagination towards all of the possible pros and cons associated with a certain idea, you begin involving the sixth sense and the subconscious mind. This technique will force the subconscious mind to search for a possible gut feeling and enhance your feeling of intuition.

Dream Wisdom

Dreams can become a powerful link to your inner intuitive mind. For many super-humans and religious leaders, the power of dreams can become a gateway for wisdom. Have you ever heard the saying, "Let me sleep on it"? This is a way for you to turn over the problem-solving task to the subconscious mind. Throughout the day and before going to bed, take some time and go over all of the possible avenues, outcomes, and choices to your problem. As you go to sleep, the subconscious mind is spinning its wheels searching through all of its available information and can sometimes show you the best solution in the form of a dream. Do not discount the powers of the subconscious mind. Use a notebook to record as much of your dream as you can remember. Sometimes the intuitive answer is hidden in the context of your dreams.

Suggestion

Sometimes we can get so wrapped-up in trying to find an answer to our problems that we actually stymie our creative genius. By using the power of self-suggestion to free up your intuitive instincts, you can be looking for answers while going about your everyday business. For example, in the morning I will write down the problem that I need solved on a piece of paper and mentally verbalize this problem to myself five times in a row. I now try to forget about this problem and go about my day as usual. While I am consciously performing my everyday tasks, my subconscious mind is actively searching its databases for the necessary information. At sometime during the day or night, a little light bulb will appear above my head and a good idea or intuitive feeling will strike me. Try condensing your problem into a single word that is the main theme for your problem. Use this central word to apply the self-suggestion technique and free up your sixth sense.

The Spirit Animal

Some North American and South American Indian cultures believe that every person has a spirit animal that best represents and guides them through life. If you are trying to figure out the puzzling actions or words of a co-worker or family member, try using this metaphor technique to gather some insight into this person's behavior. Imagine in your mind if this person was an animal, what sort of animal would he or she be? Be open to any images that suddenly come to mind.

The sixth sense will help you interpret these images into emotional and physical reasons. When you think of this person and a lion comes to mind, words like dangerous, ferocious, cunning, furry, and dominating might come to mind. Also remember that the lion can also be loving, protective, caring, and motherly. This person might appear to be confrontational and menacing, but they may also have low self-esteem and be very vulnerable. Use this age-old technique to free up your intuition about people in your everyday life.

The Sixth Sense Diary

Keep a personal journal or notebook of your gut-feelings and flashes of brilliance. This technique will help you become much more aware of your sixth sense and help you identify when your intuition is trying to tell you something. Some of your information will be trivial, while some may be more solid and fact-ridden. All of your recorded hunches attest to the activity of your sixth sense. If you observe in your journal that 25% of all your gut-feelings occurred while looking out your office window, then you might wish to invest more of your time and mental effort into creating this winning environment. Always note in your journal the time, place, activity, and atmosphere when the hunch first came to you, but also make sure to record how, when, and if that particular insight became validated.

DISCIPLINE DEFICIENCY

"Man's many desires are like the small metal coins he carries about in his pocket. The more he has – the more they weigh him down."
-Satya Sai Baba

A lack of discipline in any individual, group, or society can lead to disaster. The ability of an individual to self-manage his or her actions is proportional to the level of success and happiness they will experience in their lifetime. Self-discipline is not about punishment or even about a restrictive lifestyle. It is the ability of an individual to adhere to actions, thoughts, and behaviors that result in personal improvement instead of instant gratification. A lack of self-discipline is the main reason for the failures we experience in both our personal and professional lives. It is also the underlying reason we experience disease, obesity, financial ruin, and relationship problems on a national level.

Self-discipline is much like the operating systems we use for our computers. Systems like Windows 98 or Macintosh OS are what we use to direct and control every aspect of a computer's functions. A computer without an operating system is much like a person who lacks discipline. They both have a tremendous amount of potential and power, but have no way to function properly. Unlike a computer, we are blessed with the gift of free will, but without self-discipline we are susceptible to the viruses of instant gratification, excuses, and bad habits.

The most common and destructive virus found in our personal operating system is the justification virus. As human beings, we have the tendency to justify our poor decisions by using excuses. We use the power of excuses to justify our poor performance, our attitudes, our problems, and ultimately our lack of overall happiness.

Once we begin to consciously recognize excuses we use to justify the circumstances in our lives, we can focus our efforts towards fixing the real problem. Before we can develop the power of self-discipline, we must first take an honest and direct look at the excuses we use to justify our problems and poor daily performance. Keep in mind that as human beings we will always make mistakes and blunders, but it is through the power of self-discipline that we are able to diminish their impact on our lives.

In order to begin combating the virus of excuses, we must take a look at some of the more common problems that exist in our lives and the excuses that we use to justify them. One of the most effective methods that you can use to identify the problems that exist in your life is to make a detailed list of your problems and excuses. By writing down this information you are able to take an objective look at what viruses are effecting your personal operating system. Here is an example of some common problems that we experience and the resulting excuses we use to justify them. I encourage you to sit down and objectively think about the problems that exist in your life, and the excuses you use to justify them.

THE EXCUSE VIRUS

PROBLEM　　　　　　　　　　　　　　EXCUSE

1. Overweight　　　　　　　　"I don't have time to eat right!"

2. Procrastination　　　　　　"I can only do so much in a day!"

3. Always in debt　　　　　　　"They don't pay me enough!"

4. Stressed out　　　　　　　　"I never have time to relax!"

5. Marital conflict　　　　　　"He/she is just too demanding!"

6. Work performance　　　"If they paid me more –I'd do more!"

7. Smoking　　　　　　　　　"I need it for stress relief!"

8. Drinking　　　　　　　"One drink never hurt anybody!"

9. Diet　　　　　　　　"Who has time to prepare a meal!"

10. No daily exercise　　　　　"I just can't find the time!"

11. Anger　　　　　　　　"They had it coming to them!"

12. Depression　　　　"Nothing ever goes right for me!"

13. Poor appearance　　　　"It's the newest fashion!"

14. Divorce　　　　　　　"We just couldn't work it out!"

15. Lack of Self-discipline "I have enough things to worry about!"

This list of problems and excuses is simply an example of our inherent tendency to justify our words, actions, and behaviors. The problems we face and the methods we use to deal with them vary from individual to individual, but the underlying solution will always remain consistent. Before you can inject discipline into your personal operating system, you must take the action of personal responsibility. Get in the habit of identifying the real reason behind the circumstances in your life and defeat the excuse virus.

LET'S GET PERSONAL

"There is nothing more to be esteemed than a strong firmness and decision of character. Like a person who knows his own mind and sticks to it; who sees at once what is to be done in any given circumstance and does it now."
-James Haszlitt (1778-1830)

At some point in time, it becomes necessary to clear away all of the nice-to-know information and get down to the heart of the matter. This is such a time. It makes no difference what your background is, where you went to college, how much you earn, what job title you have, or even how old you are. What matters most is that we are all members of a certain species that share certain things in common. The human species of today has very similar needs, wants, problems, and desires that create the circumstances in our lives. In order for us to use the power of self-discipline to bring our desires into reality, we must learn more about ourselves.

The majority of people today get so caught up in the daily grind that they soon forget why they are working so fast and furious. When was the last time you took a hard look at yourself and thought about why you go to work every morning? Have you ever thought about why you dress the way you do or why you work in the field of industry that you do? Why do you feel depressed or stressed out? When was the last time you analyzed your words, thoughts, and actions to determine why you behave or think a certain way? All of these questions point to the basic wants and problems of the human species of today.

There are several basic problems and desires of today's human being, and most of our efforts are directed at meeting them. The first step to gaining control of our lives is to get personal with ourselves and determine what drives us to think and act like we do. Understand that your ability to direct and control all aspects of your life is directly proportional to your level of self-discipline. Let's take a look at seven of the major human problems and desires.

THE 7 DRIVING FORCES

Problems   ## Desires

1. "I am overworked and underpaid!"	"I want more MONEY!"
2. "I am fat and out of shape!"	"I want to be ATTRACTIVE!"
3. "My life is so hectic and stressful!"	"I want more CONTROL!"
4. "I hate my job!"	"I want a satisfying CAREER!"
5. "My personal life is a nightmare!"	"I want to be LOVED!"
6. "Nobody listens to me!"	"I want to be RESPECTED!"
7. "I just can't seem to get anywhere!"	"I want SATISFACTION!"

The fact remains that unless you are a Buddhist Monk or from another planet, you probably think, talk, and act in a certain way, because you are affected by these seven driving forces. The problems begin when we have no system of controlling and directing these driving forces. The power of self-discipline is the ability we all have that is capable of guiding these driving forces in the direction of our goals. When we take a closer look at today's society, we see the results of these seven driving forces running out of control. These powerful driving forces can become overwhelming when they are left to chance or uncontrolled. You need to look no farther than your local newspaper or the daily news show to see the results of a society that lacks the power of self-discipline.

With the advent of increasing technological wonders, the need for a personal system of checks and balances has become even more critical. We can satisfy almost any urge or impulse with the touch of a keyboard button and instant gratification has replaced long term satisfaction. In order to better understand the consequences of living without self-discipline, let's take a look at some of today's human performance statistics for the top five driving forces.

STATISTICS

1. Money

- The average American owes approximately $85,000 to creditors.
- One in every 36 Americans files for bankruptcy.
- Today's mid-level drug dealer makes $120,000 and a teacher -$30,000.
- Today's porn star makes around $250,000 and a policeman –$35,000.

2. Health

- The average American consumes over 22 pounds of sugar, 26 gallons of alcohol and 261 pounds of meat each year.
- A shocking 72% of Americans are medically overweight.
- The top three items we purchase at supermarkets are Marlboro cigarettes, Coca-Cola Classic, and Kraft Processed Cheese.
- The average American consumes approximately 3,600 calories a day. A healthy adult only requires between 2,500 and 2,700 calories a day.

3. Work

- In 1998, theft, employee error, and fraud cost 43 million dollars to the retail industry alone.
- There were 600 workplace-related murders last year.
- According to an independent survey, the average American worker actually puts in five hours of work during an eight-hour workday.

4. Control

- Every four seconds a violent crime is committed and every nine seconds a murder is committed.
- The average American watches almost four hours of TV per night.
- The top reason for murder in the United States is family arguments.
- The top two pieces of literature we read are People Magazine and TV Guide.

5. Love

- In the United States today, seven out of ten marriages will end in divorce.
- Marital violence and rape is at epidemic proportions.
- 32 million people are infected with the AIDS virus.

These statistics are not meant to leave you with the impression that everything is hopeless and beyond help. In fact, there is more good in the world than bad. However, the fact remains that we are quickly spinning out of control and need to rediscover the power of discipline before things really get crazy. Along with all of the new freedoms and wonders that technology brings into our lives, it also provides us with many more choices. It is a universal law of human nature that with more choices comes more mistakes, and with more mistakes comes greater problems in our lives.

The only answer to gaining control of our lives in this day and age is simply the human ability of personal control through discipline. So how do we define self-discipline? Well here is a good place to start. According to Webster's Dictionary, *Discipline* is defined as:

"Training that corrects, molds or perfects"
"Control gained by obedience or training."
"To train or develop by the exercise of self-control."
"A system of rules governing conduct."

From this we can gather that *Self-discipline* is:

A personal system of rules that govern our individual words, thoughts and actions. A personal system of training that establishes self-control and corrects, molds and perfects our daily performance as humans.

To see in ourselves this ability which always existed, is very difficult for the everyday man and woman. It is so easy, so enticing, so utterly pleasurable to let our minds toil and hide in everyday tasks. We decide to shut our eyes to the reality of the conditions and circumstances that we call our life. You may shake this off, wake up tomorrow and continue your present life vowing that such things don't happen to you. Yet it happens to somebody everyday. So is the plight of the everyday lamb, who fails to notice that inside lurks a predator of success. For some people, it takes nothing more than reading and understanding this concept, and for others it takes a little more. I would, if I could, come to your home and smack you on the head to engrain this in your mind.

THE POWER OF CHOICE

"No one finds life worth living; he must make it worth living by choice."
-Tibetan proverb

Everything in life is a matter of choice. There are only two things in life for which we have no choice. We cannot change these two facts of life no matter how hard we try. The first unchangeable fact is that we must die. Death is an absolute fact. The second fact, for which we have no choice over, is that we must live a certain number of years before we die. Now understand this –everything else in your life is the result of your power to choose. Everything that you say, think, wear, drive, eat, read, watch, and do is a personal choice made by you. We live in the confines of what we call "our life" because we have created this existence through our individual ability to make choices.

We cannot change the fact that we are going to die, or the fact that we must live before we die, but we can change everything else because it is a choice. Examine where you are in your life. Where you are is where you have chosen to be. Consciously or unconsciously, you have made this your life by choice. Understand that certain universal laws of nature are at play in your life. The first law is the most important law when it comes to our ability to choose the right direction. The first law states that all human beings make more wrong choices than right choices during their lifetime. Is your life working out the way you dreamed it would? Do you have the things you would like to have? Are you where you would like to be? Do you have the house, body, job, checking account, relationship, or character that you always wanted? If the answer to any of these questions is no, then let's take a look at the second universal law of nature.

The second universal law of nature simply states that all human beings have ·the power to create their own circumstances. Whether they are the circumstances you always dreamed of, or the circumstances you settle for, you are the artist and life is the canvas. No one determines if your life will be a masterpiece but you. Think about how you want your life to be. Think about what turns you on. When was the last time that you felt enthusiastic or fired up about something? Stop racing through life at 100 mph and take the time to look at how you want your life to turn out.

Most of us are trying to become successful, trying to become happy, or wealthy, or loved, or to gain something from life that is presently not there. These can be summed up as dreams, and the choices we make each day is either a step toward our dreams or a step away from them. This is the power of choice. The ability to know what you want in life, and then make correct choices based upon these wants, is called goal setting. Goal setting is simply making choices based upon a desired result. It is knowing where you want to go. If you are not achieving what you are capable of achieving, it is because your goals are not clearly defined. Having goals is one thing, but having a plan to achieve them is another. Your success in any project will be determined largely by your individual plan of action.

There is a direct connection between the power of choice and our self-worth. As we develop self-discipline and condition ourselves to make correct choices, we in turn increase our self-esteem. Self-discipline enables us to win small victories each day over our habits, urges, and compulsive behavior. The more good choices we make, the more positive our self-esteem becomes. As our self-esteem builds, we begin to develop powerful momentum in the direction of our goals.

It is essential to our personal success and happiness that we continue this chain of self-discipline, correct decision-making, and self-esteem. The power of choice is the one control mechanism we possess that advertising, television, music, and outside influence try to wrestle from us. When you see people wearing a certain popular style of clothing, or listening to a certain type of music, or eating a certain type of food, you can see the influence that society has over their power of choice. When we lack self-discipline, our ability to make correct decisions based upon our needs and wants, and not those of society, becomes very weak. Just as the chain reaction of good choices leads to increased self-esteem and self-discipline, the momentum of poor choices leads to depression, obesity, and poor daily performance. Have you ever had a bad day where you woke up and didn't feel on top of the world? You decide to skip your morning exercise session, trade a healthy breakfast for coffee and donuts, and eat fast food for lunch. By the time dinner rolls around, you feel so depressed and lethargic from your poor decisions, that you decide to plop in front of the television instead of working on your goals. The next morning you wake up feeling even more depressed and again continue with this cycle of poor choices.

I don't believe there is a person alive who has not experienced this cycle of poor decision-making at some point in their life. The development of self-discipline is the only weapon we possess to combat this inevitable fact of life. If you wish to make lasting changes in your life, instead of bouncing from one diet to another, low self-esteem to high self-confidence, and high stress to a feeling of control, you must be ready and willing to change. The power of choice must become a conscious area of focus throughout the day. It is very important to understand the impact that our daily choices have upon our lives. There is no doubt about it; you are what you choose to be. Life is made up of thousands of choices, choices made in each second of every day of your life. This, in essence, is how you create your life – by the choices you make.

The natural human tendency to justify the circumstances in our lives by placing the blame on chance, other people, or lack of time, is the direct result of low self-discipline. You must find the inner-strength to identify your own weaknesses and accept the challenge of changing them. In order to change your cycle of poor choices, you must begin admitting that you have made poor choices and not justify or side step the blame. For most people, this is a very difficult admission, but it is the necessary starting point of lasting change. If you wish to develop self-discipline and break the cycle of poor choices, you must embrace this concept. This is the only way to generate the power to accomplish what you want, reach your goals, and continue improving the quality of your life.

With over 6 billion people occupying a slot in the great human food chain, the power of choice becomes crucial to success. Those who choose to attack their dreams, those that choose to go beyond average performance, those who choose to dominate instead of follow, will effectively become the predators of success, instead of the sheep of mediocrity. Look inside yourself and see the truth behind the problems, circumstances, and situations that exist in your life. Determine right here, right now, that you do have the power to achieve your dreams, beat your habits, and break the chains of average living. You are what you choose to be. What is your choice?

MISSION #2 INSTRUCTIONS

"Rise early for the pleasures of life and limb. No lamb for the lazy wolf –no victory was ever won in bed."
-Erik-the-Red, Viking Chief, 900 AD

For Mission #2, we are going for a skydiving reconnaissance. Our overall mission is to gather intelligence from a high altitude over the country called "our brain." This country has within it many dangerous glitches that are slowly destroying the good and powerful abilities of its inhabitants. Our ability to clearly spot and define these enemies will directly result in our life's failure or success. To accomplish this mission correctly, we need to possess the ability to honestly see things for what they are, and not for what we wish them to be. Once we have discovered the negative glitches that are holding us back, we can begin the process of reprogramming. Keep in mind, the knowledge, techniques, and tools which you have learned in this chapter, are only effective if you are wanting and willing to change. This I cannot give you, for you can only give it to yourself.

In Mission #2, I am going to ask you to write down actual sentences or paragraphs. The quality of information you find out about yourself is directly proportional to how much effort you put in to this. Since I cannot be there to smack you on the head and force you to do it, you must stop and think about what the word **self-discipline** is all about. Try and think of this mission as nothing more than a written inventory of the malfunctioning parts in a computer's mainframe. This mainframe is your brain. Understand that you have the ability to program your mind for success or failure. I leave the choice up to you.

MISSION #2

> *"Knowing is not enough; we must apply. Willing is not enough; we must do."*
> *-Goethe*

If I were to ask your spouse or significant other about your bad habits, what would he/she tell me?

How many times this year have you been late for work?

Thinking back to when you were 18 years old, how different in appearance and ability is your body today?

Where would you like to be in 10 years. How much would you like in the bank, and what would you be doing most of the day?

What was the most intense mental and physical pain you have ever felt? What was your immediate mental and physical reaction like?

If a genie appeared this instant and granted you the wish to change one thing about your body, what would you choose?

If I were to ask your co-workers to tell me about one fault that you possess, what would they tell me?

Other than death, what is the worst thing that could happen to you?

Which emotion do you experience most often? Anger/ Joy/ Sadness/ Anxiety?

When you daydream, what subject or theme do you dream about most often?

What subject do you and your spouse or significant other, fight about most?

How do you unwind or relax? How much time each day do you spend relaxing?

If I were to charge you with the crime of procrastination, what would the three biggest offenses be?

Rank your personal appearance, 1-10

Would you like to work for yourself?

How often do you cry?

Rank your self-discipline, 1-10.

What one food do you eat more than others?

How organized are you and your possessions, 1-10?

Approximately, how many times do you swear or curse per day?

How do you relieve your stress?

How many times each day do you say I love you?

What work-related skill do you need help with?

How much time in the past month have you spent working on your faults?

MISSION DE-BRIEF

"It is no use saying, 'We are doing our best.' You have got to
succeed in doing what is necessary."
-Winston Churchill

Congratulations! You have just done something that you probably have never done before. Honestly critique your brain. Stop for a minute and go back to look at what you have written. This is probably the most accurate written assessment of your personality and behavior patterns, and most likely the only one you have ever done. How can that be? You will take several inventories of your refrigerator each day, but you have never taken an inventory of your brain? Have you ever thought about why there are so many psychiatrists in the world today? It is because people would rather pay someone else to take their mental inventory for them. I bet some of you are expecting some big, secret formula that you can plug all of your written answers into and out will pop the secret to your success. Nope, that is it. "That's it!" You say. "You mean to tell me that I sat down for x amount of hours and filled out your stupid questionnaire, only to find that you have no million dollar power words to offer, or at least some 30 minute instant super-life program for me?" No, I could never give you what you have just given yourself. I am only providing you with a parachute, a loaded weapon, and a set of directions, it is up to you to take the information you now have and fight the battle.

Let's take a closer look at the information you have written and what it tells us. We have found glitches in our character, thinking habits, work habits, body, thoughts, feelings, and emotions. On the other hand, we have found our dreams, goals, likes, hobbies, loves, strengths, self-esteem, confidence, depression, and basic mental performance. We now know what we need to change in order to please ourselves, our spouse, and co-workers. More importantly, we have identified areas of our mind

84

and body that need to receive an immediate injection of self-discipline. By doing this simple task, we can now focus our energy and concentration into reprogramming our destructive behavior patterns.

If you want to achieve any goal, the path is simple. Use courage to make the decision and self-discipline to master the glitches that stop you from achieving your goals. Remember that self-discipline is simply self-mastery. Before you can begin to take the path of success and happiness, you must first master your own problems and strengths. It is just as important to improve upon the things you are doing right, as it is to destroy the things that you are doing wrong. Self-discipline is the tool that must be used to enhance the positive aspects of your life and talents, or they too will wither and die. For example, in the SEAL Teams we must be able to perform many tasks and skills with great proficiency. A jack-of-all-trades and master of none. A balance must be struck among all performance related skills, or you risk a deficiency that ultimately can mean your demise.

Balance can be a deceptive word. Balance does not mean the equal application of time and energy to all tasks, but a division of time and energy that equals success in each task. In everyday life it is not so easy to detect unbalance or inefficiencies in our daily schedule. Earlier, I talked briefly about the very important skill of time management. It is just as important to have good mental management skills as it is to have good time management skills.

Mental management is nothing more than the ability to strike a balance between the use of self-discipline for our glitches and strengths. In other words, don't spend all of your time and effort on fixing your problem areas, or your strengths and attributes will be deficient. Once you are able to control the application of self-discipline in all areas of your life, noticing an imbalance is very easy. The only way to find the perfect balance is through the trial and error of your mental management

CHAPTER 3 – THE MASTERY OF CONTROL

"In reading the lives of great men, I found that the first victory they won was over themselves...self-discipline with all of them came first."

-Harry S. Truman

Self-discipline is a powerful life force that can alter existence for man virtually overnight. Self-discipline is the most powerful weapon in the everyday fight for control of your destiny. Control is the ability to direct and monitor the progression of your journey through life. The journey we choose is as individual as we are, but in order to exert control, we must have a final destination to our journey. Life's journey is simply the path we make in the effort to attain our life goals. Life goals are the end of the rainbow, the ultimate dreams we must have to fuel our desire to live. It is when we lose sight of why we get up and go to work every day that our lives start to spin out of control. In our age of fax machines,

Internet, cellular phones, fast food, and electronic living, we must work hard every conscious moment to keep control of our hectic lives. In order to begin to have some semblance of control, we must first start with self-discipline. Self-discipline is the key to not only gaining control, but to mastering and dominating the course that our lives take. In order to master control, you must first seek out the other indispensable partners that co-exist with self-discipline.

Think of your quest for life mastery as a battlefield. On this battlefield of life are countless enemies that you encounter in your ultimate journey to your life's goals. These enemies are the glitches and situations that life has placed on this battlefield, and most of them are from your own doing. In order for us to reach our ultimate life-goals, we must face and destroy the enemies that we encounter every single day. To possess the ability to face our enemies head on and win, we must first be able to identify these obstacles and have the weapons needed to destroy them. Every living and breathing person has all of the weapons and abilities to defeat his enemies in the quest for life-goals, but most people do not know how to use them. Through self-discipline we are able to focus our inherent mental and physical abilities onto the task of controlling our personal battlefield.

When you dedicate yourself to utilizing the extraordinary potential of your mind, body, and soul, you unleash powerful forces that start to immediately change all aspects of your life. When you realize that by focusing on control, self-discipline, and personal management, your confidence and zest for life begin to explode. When your confidence and zest for life increase, your passion and energy increase exponentially. It is through this chain reaction that we open up opportunity for success. When you are inspired to achieve more for yourself, your family, and your life, all of your thoughts become like a laser, your mind transcends limitations, and you become an unstoppable juggernaut bent on success.

Self-discipline gives you the ability to control your strengths and weakness, and awakens sleeping forces, talents, and desires that come alive and cause you to discover yourself to be a greater person than you ever imagined. In order to begin mastering control, we must first examine the five elements of control. These five elements are what enable us to effectively gain control of our life and steer it into the direction of our dreams and life-goals. Here are the five key-elements of life control:

1. MASTERY OF PERSONAL MANAGEMENT
2. THOUGHT CONTROL
3. PHYSICAL CONTROL
4. KNOWLEDGE CONTROL
5. MASTERY OF GOAL MANAGEMENT

MASTERY OF PERSONAL MANAGEMENT

"Man is still responsible. He must turn the alloy of modern experience into the steel of mastery and character. His success lies not with the stars, but with himself. He must carry on the fight of self-correction and discipline."
-Frank Curtis Williams

The lost art of effective personal management is used by the Navy SEALs and the special operations world to elevate ordinary men, with blind determination, to the top of the human food chain. In the teams we have a saying that pretty much sums up our desire for perfection-"To be a perfect animal is one thing, but to be a perfect predator is the highest of callings." This simple saying is a constant reminder of the desire to want more, strive harder, accept no limits, and always continue to improve. Before you can begin to see improvements in your outside world, you must first raise the standards of expectations in your inner world.

The mastery of personal management is simply effective mental discipline. Mental discipline is nothing more than managing every thought to guarantee that it is a good and useful one. Every thought that you focus in the direction of your dreams, is like slowly intensifying the amount of light in a dark room, until finally it is awash in light. The guiding principal of mastering personal management is to always put your life goals first, and then organize everything else with the sole purpose of attaining your goals.

Personal management is one of the first SEAL techniques that I was ever taught. Personal management is the dayplanner for your actions, thoughts, and life. In order to be effective as a SEAL Team operative, personal management must be the foundation upon which all other skills are built. So goes the mastery of life control. Every successful person, corporation, and country has one underlying factor that ties them all together, and that is management. The mastery of personal management is accomplished by organization. Organization of thoughts, actions, ideas, schedules, possessions, goals, and time is the task of personal management. My success and performance as a SEAL Team operative is directly proportional to my organizational skills.

Your ability to gain control of your life is a direct result of the time, effort, and methods you use to organize. Through organization we find clarity of purpose. Let me say that again in case you missed it. Through organization we find clarity of purpose. Thirty years ago, a person might have had a chance to become successful without good personal management skills, but in today's rat-race world, we must master personal management if we wish to succeed.

One technique that we utilize in the teams is called the warning order. The warning order is a brief brainstorming/organizing session that occurs once a mission has been handed down. The mission is plainly written up at the very top of the board, and then we begin to organize all other assets, ideas, and equipment that we will need to accomplish this mission. This system of management is so effective because it follows one simple rule, KISS – **K**eep **It S**imple, Stupid. This organizational system is the basis of my quest for mastery of life control.

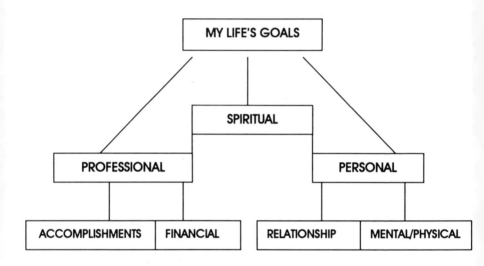

As you can see from this personal management system, I have brought order to something that is very difficult to define and control. It is through organization that the power of clarity is released, which in turn greatly increases our ability to focus on what we need to do every day to reach our goals. This organizational chart can obviously be broken down to provide much more detail about smaller goals that we try to reach in our journey for our life's ultimate goals. Personal management is the act of using self-discipline to initiate the organization and planning of our daily, yearly, and lifelong goals.

Get a briefcase, a notebook, a personal computer, or turn a wall in your house into an organizational chart with pictures included. Something that helps me in managing and visualizing my goals is pictures. I keep pictures of the place I dream of living, the type of house, my family, an example of what I want my resume to say, or anything that constantly reminds me of why I am organizing in the first place. I schedule my workouts, my eating, my sleeping, my personal time, and everything I need to do that ultimately helps me along the path to my life's goals. The mastery of personal management is one of the five elements or secrets to controlling the outcome of your life. You get out of it what you put in to it.

THOUGHT CONTROL

"The misdirected, confused, and wasted energy of everyday human life, is without a doubt –the most tragic and amusing scenc in all of nature."
-Black Elk
Medicine Man

From the moment of your birth, your first emotional experiences establish your subconscious perceptions of the world. There is not a moment of the day or night that you are not affected by your emotions. More often than not it is your programmed emotional states, not logic, that control your everyday behavior. Therefore, in order to behave a certain way or initiate certain actions, we must first learn to control our subconscious mind. Your subconscious mind flawlessly records everything your have ever done, seen, felt, heard, smelled, or tasted. However, it is not capable of interpreting the true meaning of the information it records. It simply takes the information it accumulates, divides and organizes it into separate programs that determine how you will respond to recurring circumstances and experiences in your daily life.

Once a program is formed by the subconscious mind, it will focus considerable effort to the continuation of the pre-programmed behavior or action, regardless of the consequences to your life. There are two subconscious actions that activate an emotional state, which results in a program of thoughts and actions. Think of these two different subconscious components as switches on a record system. When these switches are pulled, the subconscious mind begins to power-up and create a response. This response is an emotional state, which in return creates a mental and physical reaction causing you to think or act out a pre-programmed response.

The two trigger components of the subconscious mind are:

1. **ASKING YOURSELF A QUESTION** - The subconscious mind gives an answer followed by a picture in your mind's eye.

2. **SELF TALK** - This also activates the subconscious mind into correlating a picture, which in turn generates an emotional response and programmed behavior.

A good example of this process is when people constantly ask themselves negative questions or statements like... Why can't I make more money, Why am I so fat, I would do that if I had more time, or I am too stressed to think about that now! By asking these questions or thinking these negative statements, your subconscious mind automatically answers with negative responses such as...You wont make more money because you are in a nowhere job and you don't budget correctly. You are fat because you eat too much bad food because you are lazy and stressed. For each of these negative answers, the subconscious mind will produce a movie or picture in your mind's eye that shows you fat, overworked, underpaid, and stressed out. The mind now solidifies these pictures of negative situations and focuses incredible power towards maintaining this work and body situation. So basically, what you think and say mentally, becomes reality.

In order to gain control of your reality, you must first gain control of your thoughts. Experts estimate that your subconscious mind generates over 60,000 thoughts per day, and your inner voice speaks to you at a rate of 1,200 words per minute. However, you can only speak about 250 words per minute. So I hope you can now see just how active and powerful your subconscious mind is, and that by controlling it, you control your life. In the last chapter we discussed reprogramming your thought patterns to generate positive pictures in your mind's eye. There are several tools that we can use to begin controlling the focus of our thoughts, and begin reprogramming our desired outcome.

Substitute Thinking

This is an ancient Indian Yogi technique used to develop their tremendous mental focus. This technique employs the tactic of substituting negative thoughts for positive thoughts. The mind's eye is like a movie screen that can hold only one image at any given time. If you are disorganized, every time the thought of how all of your affairs are in disarray appears in your mind, recognize, isolate, and substitute it with a clear picture of you working hard to organize every aspect of your day. You must picture in your mind's eye the pride, efficiency, and amazing results of organizing your personal affairs. This is a direct application of disciplining and controlling your thoughts to produce a desired outcome. Every time you recognize a negative thought, I want you to use this technique to substitute a positive one and experience the power of thought control and discipline. Soon you will think of only positive behavior and actions, which will become programmed into habit.

Physical Visualization

This technique involves actually physically visualizing the results that you desire. By every day seeing a picture of the body you want to have, a picture of the house and place you wish to own, or a written statement of personal improvement, you are visually reprogramming your subconscious mind. The process of bombarding your mind with positive pictures and statements, is much like the medical application of radiation to bombard and destroy cancer cells. Think of the negative thoughts in your mind as a cancer, and the process of physical visualization as radiation treatment. Start by taping pictures and statements to your mirrors, car dash, home and work walls, and any place that you spend a lot of time. Take pictures from magazines, books, and whatever else you can find that best represent your desired goals. Go out and by a yellow sticky pad, and begin writing down positive statements like, " I will run one mile today to burn away my disgusting fat," or "I will better manage my time to improve my job performance." Once you know what the desired outcomes are in your life, it is very simple to begin having them by utilizing these two techniques to gain control of your thoughts and reality.

PHYSICAL CONTROL
"Control your physical activity, or it will control you."
-Chinese adage

Physical control is the mastery of physical management. Physical management is the art of organizing exercise, diet & nutrition, appearance, and cleanliness into a powerful force for longevity, health, and success. The powerful and wondrous force of physical control is a direct reflection and product of self-discipline. Your physical presence is the picture and impression you give every day to your family, friends, co-workers, and fellow human beings. How you look and feel physically is a direct reflection on your competence. I am not talking about the definition of beautiful or handsome, rather the idea of care, maintenance, performance, and self-esteem. The reason that physical control and thought control are so closely related is because you cannot change one without the other.

The ability to feel healthy, vibrant, clean, able, and full of energy is in direct correlation to your self-discipline. How you present yourself in everyday life, whether it is at home or at the office, is simply the ability to personally control your appearance, words, and actions. Once we have programmed the mind to think and focus on positive thoughts, we must now put it into our outward presentation.

How does one master physical control? Through the use of personal management and thought control. The ability to organize and manage your time is a fantastic power, but without scheduling time for physical management, it is useless. For example, let's say you have mastered the skills of personal management and thought control to the point that you now have lots of free time every day to spare, and you use that spare time to work on your personal projects instead of physical control. Every day at work you show up out of shape, ungroomed, unkept, late, and with a wrinkled suit on. Do you really think that people will notice how well organized and positive you now are? What sort of message are you sending to your co-workers, customers, and boss about your level of competence and determination?

The one underlying factor of the five elements to life control is balance. Without having balance between the five elements, you start to create deficiencies. By making a conscious decision to generate an appearance of professionalism, pride, and competence, you begin to reap the benefits of life control. We all know that the appearance of health, vitality, cleanliness, and confidence generates a feeling of attractiveness and discipline. So in order to begin benefiting from our newfound self-discipline, we must begin to advertise and display the outward results of our transformation.

BENEFITS OF PHYSICAL CONTROL

1. Enhanced energy and stamina.
2. A sharp, crisp, and professional appearance.
3. A significant increase in focus, determination, and creativity.
4. Lower sleep requirements.
5. A longer and more pleasure-filled life.
6. Enhanced memory, alertness, and mental aptitude.
7. A greater sense of confidence and self-worth.
8. A dramatic improvement in family, work, and life performance.
9. Becoming an example of self-discipline for all to see.
10. Revitalized feeling of purpose and accomplishment.

AREAS TO APPLY PHYSICAL CONTROL

1. **Early to bed and early to rise.** Nothing improves your performance like preparation. Plan your day before you go to bed, and get up early to prepare yourself.
2. **Have the look of a self-discipline master.** Start with a crisp and well-tailored appearance. Groom your hair and features. Walk with a purpose. Advertise your professionalism.
3. **A healthy body enhances the healthy mind.** Pay attention to the next chapter. Investigate and acquire the knowledge of nutrition. Move with agility and strength. Study vitamins, supplements, herbs, and healthy lifestyles.
4. **Organization is infectious.** Start preparing schedules, to do lists, and attacking them. Organize and clean your home, office, vehicles,

and other possessions. Manage a balance between your professional and personal life. Start a journal, get an organizer or dayplanner.

5. **Cleanliness is next to Godliness**. Find the time to shower twice a day. Smell good and clean. Work on unsightly bad habits. Eat clean foods. Take pride in your possessions.

Assume the responsibility of personal control and appearance, and everyone will notice the benefits. Come to love and care about the body that God has given you, and you will be well on your way to happiness and longevity.

KNOWLEDGE CONTROL

"Know all things to be desired: a mirage, a cloud castle, a dream, an apparition without essence, but with qualities that can be obtained."
-The Tibetan Book of Living and Dying

The art of knowledge control is not the restriction or condemnation of information mediums, but rather the selection, filtering, and focusing of life enhancing information and knowledge. In today's society a person could spend his entire life studying, watching, and listening to the various types of information available, and still never even scratch the surface of what is out there. The idea of knowledge control is based upon the fact that almost anything we can conceive has already been written, done, talked about, and covered to a varying degree. By discovering what we want out of our personal, professional, financial, physical, and mental lives, we can now begin to learn from the people who have greatly excelled in these different areas of life.

As Americans, we have developed the extremely negative habit of narrowing our perception and knowledge base. Our country and society has only been in existence for about 220 years, yet we fail to understand and truly appreciate the contributions and information already provided for us by cultures that have been in existence for over 5,000 years. The sages, yogis, and monks of the Far East had mastered the powers of both the body and mind long before our continent was even discovered. Various ancient societies have uncovered the secrets to nutrition, medicine, spirituality, inner peace, and longevity, yet we choose to ignore or disregard this information in exchange for immediate satisfaction.

If your goals in life include wealth, health, enhanced spirituality, and professional success, we must find out who did it the best and how they achieved it. This idea is the basis for the element of knowledge control. The ability to focus our knowledge base in the area or areas we wish to enhance. If one of my life's goals is to become a wealthy man in my profession, then I must focus my input of information to center around several people who became wealthy in my profession. The same principal must hold true for all other aspects of my life. You must begin to learn all you can about the people who have dominated various aspects of human nature and success. Why spend three hours a day staring into a television screen when you can be educating yourself about the world's most successful ideas, concepts, and people.

The art of successful imitation is the process of borrowing knowledge from another's success. This is not necessarily the act of choosing a role model to mold your life after, but taking the best skills, knowledge, attributes, and characteristics of the world's most successful people. Success is not always synonymous with wealth and power, as some of the wealthiest and most powerful people have little to offer for successful imitation. Having a role model in life is important, but it is very limited in comparison to mastering successful imitation.

The element of knowledge control is simply the process of focusing your educational efforts and energy into the study of success in life. Ten years ago when I was a young SEAL, a wise old master-chief took me aside and said, "Young man, if you want to succeed and stay alive in the teams, become the shadow of those that are living and succeeding. Life is just too short to re-invent all of the mistakes that have already been made. Now get your stupid, lazy back to work!" From that day on I listened, studied, and imitated the actions and characteristics of some of the most competent and focused men in the world.

Think of knowledge control and successful imitation as the process of building the perfect human. I want you to imagine that a genie has appeared in front of you and granted you the ability to have the characteristics and skills of the ten most influential and successful men and women since the beginning of recorded history. All that you have to do is tell the genie what you want and whom you want it from. This is how we begin to master the art of knowledge control. The three keys to knowledge control are:

1. **Imitate the successful journey of great people.**
2. **Educate from their knowledge.**
3. **Initiate your own journey.**

KNOWLEDGE = ACTION = POWER

Health & Wisdom	Far Eastern philosophy, diet, medicine
Wealth & Power	American business, politics, investments
Spirituality	American Indians, Far Eastern philosophy
Physical Achievement	Olympic athletes, Martial Arts, Yoga
Art & Literature	European art, American classics
Human Nature	American psychology, Indian philosophy
Courage & Valor	Wars & Combat, American Indians, Slavery
Self-Discipline	Special Operations Units, Far East Philosophy

FOCUSING YOUR KNOWLEDGE

"The quality of a person's life is in direct proportion to their commitment to excellence, regardless of their chosen field of endeavor".
-Vince Lombardi

In order to reach our goals we need a path and a plan. The ability to formulate a plan and choose the proper path is through knowledge and experience. In order to attain both, we must study and imitate the successful journeys of those who have gone before us. Below, I want you to think about each characteristic, the person whom you feel best exemplifies that characteristic, and then begin to study everything you can about their failures and successes. The secrets of mastering your dreams are out there waiting to be discovered and imitated.

CHARACTERISTIC	*MASTER*
1. Financial Wealth	_____
2. Courage	_____
3. Hono	_____
4. Discipline	_____
5. Spirituality	_____
6. Love & Devotion	_____
7. Humility	_____
8. Physical Greatness	_____
9. Health & Longevity	_____
10. Mental Greatness	_____

MASTERY OF GOAL MANAGEMENT

"Destiny is no matter of chance. It is a matter of choice: It is not a thing to be waited for, it is a thing to be achieved."
-William Jennings Bryan

The world's most successful people, from leaders of countries to parents that have a healthy, happy, and loving family, all share a single powerful habit. The ability to set goals. Without a solid life plan and precisely defined goals, your life becomes the daily grind that has neither meaning nor purpose. Think of your life as a ship upon the sea and the habit of goal management, a complete navigation system.

The early years of your life are like the building of a great ship. This great ship is carefully and meticulously pieced together over time with the information and experiences of your childhood. How sea-worthy your vessel is depends upon a great many factors and situations, but it is never too late to re-build your ship. During our teenage years we began to prepare our ship for its launch, and for most of us there was no planned destination, just the intense desire to get away. The point we are at now in our lives is a direct result of how much useless cargo we have picked up along the way, and our ability to set goals or navigate. The process of mastering self-discipline is like that of rebuilding our ship, we throw out all the harmful and useless junk, fix the leaking holes, and install a new and powerful navigation system that will take us swiftly to our goals.

The mastery of goal management is nothing more than knowing where we want to go, creating a map to get there, and using personal management skills to navigate safely. By mastering self-discipline we are able to keep afloat when we hit some rocks or need to weather the storms of life. A life without goals is one that leads to little productivity and personal effectiveness, but also provides little happiness and even less fulfillment.

In the SEAL Teams we are paid to reach certain goals that are set by our country. These goals can be rather simple or extremely difficult, and every American feels results of our failures and successes. Our goals come in the form of missions, and our ability to master goal management directly determines if we fail or succeed. This same concept can be applied to your life goals or mission, but the only way that you will succeed in accomplishing your mission, is to first know exactly what your mission is. To have any lasting success or life control, you must plan your mission in advance. Plan for the attainment of your dreams and prepare yourself to deal with the obstacles that life puts in your path. It is imperative that you take the time to carefully think about what it is you want in life, conduct a thorough inventory of what you now have, and begin to reprogram yourself to master self-discipline for your journey.

Obtaining self-mastery and happiness will only come about when you set precise objectives for every area of your life. Successful people and top performers know exactly where they are going emotionally, mentally, physically, and financially. If you cannot see what it is you want, how can you find the path to get there? The act of using self-discipline to set and regularly review your life's goals, will allow your mind to see opportunities that will fulfill your desires. The mastery of goal management gives you the ability to live your dreams and pack far more enjoyment into your life.

A technique we use in the special operations world to help us reach our goals is called mission planning. This is a time-proven format we use to organize, delegate, and prepare ourselves for the process of attaining our goal, or accomplishing our mission. Mission planning is enacted once we have a mission statement, or a brief description of our goal. A mission statement is nothing more than a sentence that spells out exactly what it is we are to do. Mission planning is the technique we use to empower ourselves with the knowledge and tools needed to accomplish this goal. This technique can be used in everyday life to help us organize and begin the journey of reaching our life's dreams. The most important concept of life mastery that you must be able to grasp, is the concept of having and knowing a life mission statement. Simply put, you must know exactly what it is in life that you desire.

Having what you want in life is a goal that you must start working towards today. Creating the life you want to have 15 years from now must begin here, this hour, this minute, or you will drift aimlessly through life with no direction or purpose. Below are the five golden rules of life mission planning that will focus your energy towards achieving your dreams.

5 Golden Rules of Life Mission Planning

1. **Define Your Dreams.** Discover and mentally visualize the achievements, toys, job, home, career, family life, and anything else that you desire, and begin to write these down. The greatest advice ever given to me was – discover in life what it is you like to do, and then figure out how to get paid doing it. Begin to focus your concentration on thinking deeply about where you want to be in 1, 5, 10, 15, and 30 years from now. You are now defining your dreams.

2. **Develop a Battle Plan.** Now that you know what you want from life, you must begin to develop a strategy that includes deadlines. Once you begin to clearly see the path that you wish to travel, your days and their activities take on a whole new meaning. Your life now becomes filled with focus, passion, and purpose, but you must develop a plan, attach deadlines, and apply self-discipline techniques in order to gain clarity. Your goals must be broken down into smaller and smaller bits to become manageable and to gain confidence. Start

using the techniques of personal management to organize and develop a strategy, which begins with small steps and ends with your supreme goals.

3. **Thought Domination.** Allow your goals and strategies to dominate your thoughts and actions. Spend 90% of your time and energy working towards these goals by utilizing visualization and mental self-discipline to help develop ideas and strategies for achievement. By thinking non-stop of the realization of your dreams, you develop a remarkable belief and determination that will truly amaze you. The self-disciplined person expects success. Every morning begin by thinking of how you will look, feel, and act when all of your dreams and desires become reality. Picture the happiness and joy you will feel at the end of your life, knowing that you have mastered personal success and reached your goals.

4. **Persistence = Power.** Remember that if you can do anything for 14 days, you have begun to develop a life-changing habit. When things go wrong or not as you have planned, stick with it and fight through the battle with persistence. Through the process of programming yourself to master self-discipline, you begin building the foundation of persistence, and with this you wield the power of flexibility. Condition yourself to pick up the pieces when things fall apart, failure is nothing except the process of brushing yourself off and learning from mistakes. Persistence is what separates the successful people from the almost-successful people.

5. **Have Fun.** Treat yourself to the sweet rewards of everyday life, and stop along the journey to success to truly enjoy the gift of breathing. It is the small victories in life that generate the power to win the large

victories. Master self-discipline by reflecting on what you did right and wrong, be hard on yourself and life will be easy on you. Remember that it is peace of mind that you are searching for, but do not get so caught up in the process that you forget the small pleasures in life. Reward yourself for attaining the small goals, but learn from errors and practice self-discipline to make sure they do not happen again. Enjoy feeling productive, focused, and truly happy. Learn to become the creator of your destiny, to gain control, and navigate your ship to the Promised Land with self-discipline.

MISSION #3 INSTRUCTIONS

"You can't wake a person who is pretending to be asleep".
-Navajo Proverb

For Mission #3, I want you to imagine that you are a Navy SEAL sniper. As a sniper you are outfitted with the most sophisticated cameras, night vision, weapons, recording and communication equipment that money can buy. You once again are inserted into the chaotic country called "Your Life", and the battle for life-mastery depends upon your success in this mission. For this mission you are to observe, record, and communicate all of the prospective targets that we wish to attain. These targets are actually your dreams and desires, and must be discovered, monitored, explored, and recorded for us to use in the battle for life-mastery.

I want you to close your eyes and picture yourself looking through a pair of clear binoculars. With these binoculars we are searching the terrain of our minds for the targets or desires we wish to have in our life. Once spotted we will focus and concentrate our mind's binoculars on each and every desire we encounter. Once we have spent hour upon hour searching and focusing on these desires, we must now begin to record exactly what it is we see.

This mission is designed to force you to really take a deep look into your mind, and find out what it is you really want from life. It can be anything that you want, big or small, these are yours and yours alone. Before you fill out the worksheet or begin moving ahead, I want you to stop what you are doing and put this book down. Now, I want you to walk away and begin thinking about what you really want out of life, and what really makes you happy now and in the future. Remember that you get out of this what you put in to it, so I will tell you again – take your time and think about your dreams and desires. You are cheating no one except yourself if you will not do some serious soul-searching.

MISSION #3

"Half the failures of this world arise from pulling in one's horse as he is leaping".
-Augustus Hare

I want you to write down the top five personal character goals that you wish to have accomplished for this year and their time limits. These goals are things about you as a person that you wish to change or strengthen, to the point that they are your most distinct character traits. Stop and think about the weaknesses and personality glitches that you want and need to overcome.

THERE IS NO PURSUIT MORE NOBLE THAN MASTERING YOURSELF AS A HUMAN BEING. EVERY DAY IT IS EXTREMELY IMPORTANT THAT YOU SET ASIDE TIME TO RELAX YOUR MIND, YOUR BODY, RETREAT, RE-FOCUS, AND GAIN CLARITY OF PURPOSE.

The art of mastering self-discipline is not a journey of sacrifice or deprivation, but one of control and focus. The power to manage, understand, and focus your physical and mental talents towards a set goal or lifestyle is not meant to restrict or deprive an individual of pleasure and fun, but rather to enhance these experiences. The object of mastering self-discipline is to increase the amount of pleasure and decrease the amount of pain your experience, through the process of controlling your thoughts, actions, emotions, and future.

The long journey to attaining your goal must above all things be full of fun, pleasure, health, and enjoyment. The old adage of work hard and play hard still applies in life, but a better way to look at this journey is to work smarter and play more. It is just as important to set pleasure and fun goals for your life as it is to set professional and work goals, but the true trick to mastering personal management is to balance and focus on both.

Goals are the foundation to a lifetime of achievement and personal excellence. In order to begin the process of attaining our goals, we must first have a burning desire or personal drive towards having more than the ordinary life. Everybody dreams of having wealth, power, health, and a lifetime of pleasure, but few people ever attain this level in life because they never learn how to focus on their goals. Just by writing your goals down on paper, you have enacted the powerful force of imagination, which is the lifeblood of reality. You have now set goals that will provide thought, desire, and clarity for your quest to mastering control of your life. Most people wake up every day not having any idea of where their life is going. By accomplishing this mission you have now developed a personal vision - quest. You can now see clearly the destination of your journey. Reality does not happen with out focus and persistence, so maintain constant energy towards your goals. Master personal control, reach for your goals and have the destiny that you choose.

MISSION DE-BRIEF

"If, before going to bed every night, you will tear a page from the calendar, and remark, there goes another day of my life, never to return, you will become time conscious."
-A. B. Zu Tavern

At this point, I hope that you are still not looking for that instant success formula, or million-dollar phrase that will bring the power of self-discipline into your life. You have already taken the first step to learning how to master self-discipline by reading and taking the responsibility of doing a little soul-searching. The missions that you have accomplished so far, are methods of creating an environment of personal management and clarity of purpose. It is extremely important that you understand and honestly think deeply about what all of this information means to you. In order to start implementing self-discipline into your life, you must first go through the process of determining what areas of your life need it the most.

In the SEAL Teams, the process of developing strategies to attain goals is a never-ending necessity. This goal development process is what creates self-discipline and self-discipline in turn, creates goal development. You must understand that the ability to master self-discipline is gained by winning one small battle at a time. Tackle small personal goals first and develop your own set of strategies from these small victories. One of the most powerful concepts that I have learned from my years in the special operations world, is that every human being has the ability to control their environment, life, and destiny. In order to start making things right, you must first learn exactly what is wrong.

Once you have read and completed this book, you will posses an instruction manual for your existence. The information that is contained in this instruction manual must be read and re-read often, but with clarity and conviction.

Now that you know what it is you want from life, I want you to find pictures, books, magazines, and whatever else will give you a visual picture of your dreams and desires. Buy yourself a pad of small post-it notes and write down all of your goals on these, then start placing them in areas that you see everyday. Remember that you must focus 90% of your energy and time thinking and acting upon your strategies, the other 10% on relaxing and preparing yourself for another day.

CHAPTER 4 - THE BATTLE OF THE BODY

"Hidden within each of us is an extraordinary force. Physical and mental discipline are the triggers that can unleash it. Exercise is a form of re-birth, when you finish a good workout, you don't simply feel better –you feel better about yourself."

-George Allen

You possess the ability to transform and elevate your life to a far greater existence from one small activity, - exercise. In today's society, people use surgery, chemicals, lasers, deadly toxins, and bizarre diets to take the path of least resistance towards winning the battle of the body. Billions of dollars a year are spent towards finding the secret miracle cure that gives humans a healthy, energetic, and visually appealing body. Every successful executive, world leader, peak performer, and athlete, all have one thing in common. The ability to understand the tremendous power of daily physical exercise as a tool for self-mastery, and a life of superior excellence. The most amazing example of our inherent human tendency to take the path of least resistance, can be found in the very fact that we spend billions of dollars searching for the secret to health, vitality, beauty, and success when the answer is right there in front of us. The secret that I speak about is the most basic foundation of human existence, and that secret is daily physical exercise.

Physical exercise is the key that unlocks the door to wealth, power, longevity, sex, beauty, and a lifetime of happiness. If something as simple as exercise can be the answer to all of our dreams and desires, why don't most people include it in their lives? The answer is simple. Physical exercise requires effort, time, and self-discipline. So you say that you are just too busy to exercise. If you truly are busy, then you cannot afford not to exercise. Sit down and make one of the best decisions of your life and commit yourself to a daily exercise routine. If you are already involved in a fitness routine, step up and take it to the next level or start competing in the sport of your interest.

Physical exercise will propel you to a superior life quicker than any other strategy or technique known to man. It is absolutely free for you to achieve and can be exceptionally fun and powerful if you approach it with the right attitude. Once you begin a consistent exercise program, you will become so used to it that it turns into a daily habit like eating or waking up. Physical exercise is like the fountain of youth, in that it is more addicting than drugs and allows you to slow down the aging and dying process of your body. When you make the commitment to include daily physical exercise into your day, all aspects of your life will improve including your mental sharpness, physical appearance, social relationships, and overall happiness. Here I have listed the four things that you must sacrifice or give to exercise, and the ten things that exercise gives back to you in return.

GETTING WHAT YOU NEED

WHAT YOU GIVE	*WHAT YOU GET*
Time	Lifetime of Health
Energy	Longevity of Life
Sweat	Unlimited Energy
1 Hour of Effort	Enhanced Mental Capacity
	Enthusiasm & Confidence
	Resistance to Stress
	Beautiful Body & Spirit
	Enhanced Personal Sex Life
	Less Illness & More Life
	Discipline in All Areas of Life

I hope this provides clarity to the pain you will suffer over the rest of your life from not including physical exercise in your daily schedule, and the powerful benefits you are destined to receive from making this your #1 priority each day. Most people have the misconception that exercise must involve pain, heavy weights, running long distances, and beating up your body, but this notion could not be further from the truth. Some far-East cultures have been practicing and perfecting organized systems of physical exercise that are not only serene and pleasant, but graceful and beautiful to watch.

The physical exercise systems of Yoga, Tai Chi, and traditional martial arts all improve your stamina, flexibility, relaxation, and mental focus powers. These systems, when combined with a healthy diet and persistence, will have a dramatic effect on the quality and quantity of your life. Simple activities such as brisk walking, bicycle riding, swimming, and running are exercises that can be done by young and old alike. By doing some form of physical exercise each day, you will stay younger longer, become much more productive, eliminate stress, and generate a powerful spirit of vitality.

When you step up and make the decision to exercise, you must remain persistent, consistent, and motivated in your scheduled program to receive real, everlasting results. In just one week, a vibrant energy will radiate into all areas of your life and you will feel better than you have ever felt before. No matter what form of exercise you choose to undertake, you will feel the powerful increase of personal energy in all areas of your life. The feelings of weakness, fatigue, and complacency will disappear when you come home from a long day of work. Instead you will have the energy and desire to take part in productive activities that are sure to improve the overall quality of your life. Below I have listed 10 techniques to help you stay motivated and committed to daily physical exercise.

1.   **Create a realistic schedule and stick to it**

2.   **Start off slow (20 minutes a day) and think positive thoughts**

3.   **Visualize what your new body will look like**

4.   **Include a partner with similar goals**

5.   **Have a playful attitude and have fun**

6.   **Mix up your exercises and sports**

7.   **Use knowledge control, read books and magazines about exercise**

8.   **Keep a daily log of your progress and accomplishments**

9.   **Stand on the scale and look in the mirror often**

10.   **Use music as a motivator, buy a walkman, get excited**

Make a dramatic change in your life. Become motivated, energized, and excited about each and every day. Wake up with power, focus, and clarity about your journey to achieving all that you desire. You are not stupid, and this is so very simple. Can you honestly justify not setting aside 1 out of the 24 hours in a day to increase your life span, mental clarity, and overall happiness? What is it going to take; disease, illness, insecurity, or a shotgun to get you off of the couch and into a physical exercise program? You can give me and everyone else, all of the excuses you want, but ultimately you cannot fool yourself.

SPECIAL OPERATIONS PHYSICAL MASTERY

*"Before the gates of excellence the high gods have placed
sweat; long is the road thereto and rough and steep at first; but
when the heights are reached, then there is ease, then there is
ease, though grievously hard in the winning."*
-Hesiod

In the elite world of the Navy SEALs, acts of physical greatness and wonder are as normal as waking up is for most people. Basic Underwater Demolition Seal School is the most intense physically and mentally demanding training in the world. With a failure and dropout rate of nearly 85%, SEAL training pushes men to the extreme limits of the body and mind. Physical exercise and training is what we utilize to transform men into skillful and thoughtful predators. Most people never take the opportunity to push their minds and body to the limit, to see exactly what they are made of. Before you begin thinking that our methods of exercise are Neanderthal and torturous, let me point out that the SEAL Teams physical exercise systems are considered by most experts to be on the cutting edge of physical science and technology.

The techniques and information that I will share with you are designed to be customized to an individual's needs, age, physique, and lifestyle. The techniques and exercise that you will learn are designed to strengthen and limber every muscle group in the human body. It is important to point out that if you have a weak area, or past injury to a certain body part, you must slowly and carefully begin to focus on strengthening and limbering this area. It is not the purpose of this book to become another dissertation on the subject of exercise, but to provide you with a foundation upon which to begin mastering physical control.

In the following pages you will find simple yet powerfully effective techniques and exercises that will help in dramatically changing the way you live life. Remember that your main objective is to enhance the quality of your life and begin learning the principals of mastering physical discipline. It is imperative that you start out slow and easy at first, then increase the effort and repetitions as you gain more confidence and power.

In the SEAL Teams we have five simple and effective principals of physical exercise that we use as the foundation of all physical related activities. These five principals are designed to maximize the effects that physical exercise has upon the human body. It makes no difference what your exercise program is, the use and understanding of these five principals will ensure the safe and immediate elevation of your physical stature. The goal of any exercise program is to enhance performance and health. Each person is unique in terms of what they wish to gain from exercise, but one factor always remains constant, and that is you must do something often.

THE 5 PRINCIPALS OF PHYSICAL EXERCISE

"Security is mostly a superstition. It does not exist in nature, nor do the children of men as a whole experience it. Avoiding danger is no safer in the long run than outright exposure. Life is either a daring adventure or nothing."
-Helen Keller

1. Overload

The basis of this principal is that the level of exercise must increase gradually to bring about various physical changes. When your body adapts to a higher level of physical exercise, it will perform more efficiently and with greater ease. Overload is initiated by increasing the intensity, duration, frequency, and style of the exercise. By increasing these aspects of exercise, you in turn increase your cardiovascular capacity and muscular strength.

2. Individuality

The results of certain types of exercises can differ from one individual to the next. By customizing the exercises to meet your personal goals and expectations, you are better able to find out what does and doesn't work for you. Expand your knowledge base to include Yoga, Tai Chi, and various other forms of physical exercise to allow yourself more choices.

3. Target Training

This principal reflects specific result-based training. By targeting a specific type of exercise to enhance a desired outcome, you begin focusing on a certain desired result. For example, weightlifting increases muscle mass and muscle group strength, but will not necessarily increase your running ability and vice versa. Therefore, it

116

is important to focus on certain muscles involved in a specific type of exercise to receive enhanced performance benefits.

4. Consistency

Physical exercise is not a task or chore, but a purposeful habit. You can make all of the excuses that you want, but you have to exercise with consistency in order to see results. By utilizing the tools of personal mastery and self-discipline, you generate the power of consistency and organization. Stop the excuses!

5. FITT = Frequency, Intensity, Type and Time

The FITT principle must be included to extract the most benefit from your exercise program. The time you spend exercising and the type of exercises you perform, are just as important as the amount and intensity of your effort. If you are not improving or enhancing, you are simply stagnating.

PERSONAL PHYSICAL RELIGION

"No man or woman has achieved an effective personality who is not self-disciplined. Such discipline must not be an end in itself, but must be directed to the development of resolute Christian character."
-John S. Bonnell

In the special operations community we use calisthenics as the primary building block for a balanced, proportional, and overall powerful body. Calisthenics is a word used to describe a series of exercises that focus on building muscular strength and flexibility for every major muscle group found in the body. In today's society of million-dollar gyms, thigh-masters, fancy machines, and spandex, calisthenics bring the individual back to the basics. Most people think that you have to become a member of a high-dollar gym or wear hundred dollar outfits to get in shape. Calisthenics allow you to get in touch with your body and mind by eliminating all of the confusion and easy-way-out philosophies that are found in today's physical fitness information.

In the SEAL Teams, we have developed calisthenics into a philosophy of personal mastery that involves relaxation, visualization, nature, mental control, and self-discipline. As elite commandos, we view our individualized calisthenics program to be more of a religion than an exercise. This "personal physical religion" is a customized program of powerful mental and physical techniques and exercises that enhance all aspects of an individual's life. The church for this personal religion is found in a quiet, serene, and motivating place. You must find an area in your backyard, local park, or house that you can turn into your personal church. Your personal exercise church must become an area of power, reflection, motivation, and goal acquisition. By adding mirrors, motivating pictures and statements, music, and a pleasing environment, your personal church becomes a place of mental and physical empowerment.

The object of a personal physical religion is to provide you with the ability to strengthen your body and mind in an individually-created environment of power. I will give you the exercises and techniques that you need to achieve physical mastery, but it is up to you to find or create the perfect environment in which to do them. While you are performing these exercises, focus your mind to generate positive thoughts and pictures about your body. You must visualize your muscles getting bigger, tighter, and stronger as you perform these exercises. Use music and pictures to stimulate your mind and body to take on an air of positive energy. Remember that the magic secret to personal success and mastery

is found in the basic personal religion of physical exercise, to use this
hour, day, and week to create a new life

BACK – BICEPS – FOREARMS

Exercise Description

Place hands about shoulder-width apart on
the bar with a reverse grip. Your palms
should be facing you with the thumb
wrapped around the bar. Begin at a dead
hang and slowly pull entire body upwards
until your chin is above the bar. Pause for
approximately 2 seconds in this position,
then slowly lower to the full extension of
your arms. Repeat until exhaustion.

Chin-Ups

Standard Close-Grip Wide-Grip

These three variations of the
pull-up target all of the
muscles in the back. Rotate
your grips between standard,
close-grip, and wide grip. Pull
the body up until your chin is
above the bar, then pause and
lower slowly. It is important
to stay as still and straight as
possible, do not buck or kip
your body up.

Technique

It is extremely important that you perform these exercises with a slow and steady rhythm. Do as many of each that you can and stretch out your back after each set of pull-ups. I like to put a motivational picture or statement directly in front of me on the wall to keep my head straight and provide inspiration at the same time. Your grip, forearm, and back become strong and defined.

CHEST – SHOULDERS – ARMS

Exercise   **Description**

The diamond push-up is done by placing the hands on the ground with the thumbs touching. Keep the head and back straight as you lower you body and touch your hands with your chest.

Wide Grip - Standard

Diamond Push-Ups

The wide grip push-up is done by placing the hands as far apart as you can comfortably handle. The standard is done with the hands placed shoulder length apart. Rotate between all three of these push-ups to ensure a balanced and strong chest, shoulders, and arms.

Dive bomber push-ups build and strengthen the chest, arms, shoulders, and lower back. Spread your feet and hands shoulder-length apart. Raise your buttocks into the air, then slowly sweep your chest downward then upwards. With your lower abdomen almost touching the ground and your arms locked out, pause and reverse this motion to reset the exercise. The dive bomber push-up can be used to strengthen the forearm and grip muscles by raising your body up with your fingers extended.

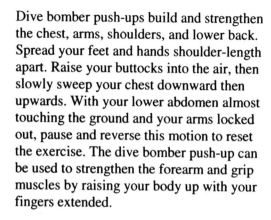

It is important to slowly perform each exercise with control and form. Do not let your body cheat when you feel the burn, simply lean to one side and shake out each arm. This exercise is a super muscle builder.

Dive Bombers

ABDOMINALS – LOWER BACK

Exercise Description

The muscle groups of the abdomen and lower back complement each other by providing support and flexibility. In order to have a strong back, you must first have a strong abdomen and vice versa. When doing exercises for the abdomen, it is important to understand the range of effective motion. If you go past 90 degrees in an exercise, you are resting and not working the abdomens. The range of motion for the lower back is only 30 degrees, so be careful not to go past this.

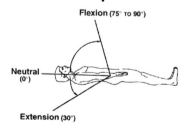

ɔtural Human Range of Motion

To lessen the amount of strain placed on the lower back during abdominal exercises, place a rolled up towel underneath the lower back. Spread your feet about shoulder length apart and concentrate on slowly raising your upper torso with your head straight up. Focus on keeping your feet firmly planted and steady.

Arms at Sides   Arms across Chest

Arms behind Head   Arms above Head

Abdominal Sit-up Variations

These 4 sit-up variations allow you the opportunity to experiment with various points of balance. It is important to keep your back perfectly straight and allow your abdomen to take on a burning sensation. Keep your motion slow and focus on moving nothing except your upper torso. To get the greatest benefit from each of these positions, allow yourself a rest period between sets.

Exercise   Description

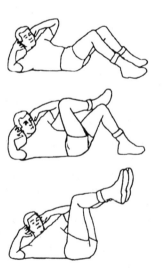

Crunches/Cross Overs

The cross over abdominal exercise is designed to individually target the left and right group of abdominal muscles. The standard crunch is designed to target the entire abdominal muscle group, but strict form is required to successfully strengthen this area. Form and strict, slow motion is the key to working the abdominal muscles for any of these crunch/cross over variations. Make sure that your legs do not move forward to meet your upper *torso*. The upper torso must remain straight and stable while moving upward to meet the lower torso.

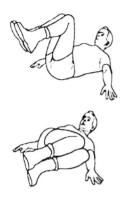

The hip roller exercise is designed to target the oblique muscles. The starting position is with the knees facing forward. While keeping your upper torso flat on the ground, lower your knees to one side and then the other. Slow and strict form is the key to getting the most out of this exercise. Focus on keeping your legs together and your back on the ground. This exercise will provide a powerful burn for your midsection when done properly.

Hip Rollers

Exercise

Description

The 8-count body builder exercise is designed to target the entire body. The eight steps to this exercise are: 1.Start in standing position. 3.Standing to squat position. 3.Squatting to push-up position. 4. Perform one push-up. 5. Simultaneously spread legs apart. 6. Simultaneously bring legs together. 7. Back to squatting position. 8. Squatting to standing position. This sequence of movements targets all of your body's major muscle groups. Increase the repetitions and speed as your confidence level rises. When done properly, this exercise generates a good muscle fatigue burn.

8-Count Body Builders

Flying Flutter Kicks

The flying flutter kicks work the lower back and buttock area. This exercise is performed while lying on your stomach and with your feet and hands off of the ground. To get the most out of this exercise, focus on keeping your chest and thighs off of the ground. The pelvic area is the balance point for this exercise. A soft foam pad helps in reducing discomfort when performing this exercise and keeps your body off of the ground. Strict and slow form is required to isolate this muscle group.

Exercise   **Description**

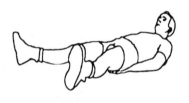

Good Morning Darlings

This exercise is designed to target the upper and inner leg muscles along with the lower abdominal muscles. Place your hands under your buttocks to provide a stable platform. Start with your legs out in front of you and about 3 inches off of the ground. Next, open your legs as far as you can, while keeping them off of the ground. Bring your legs back together to complete a repetition. It is important that you keep your legs and feet off of the ground throughout the entire exercise.

Leg Levers

Leg levers target the lower abdominal and quadriceps muscle area. Place your hands under your buttock and keep your legs about 3 inches off of the ground. Slowly raise and lower your legs from 3 inches to about 2 feet off of the ground. This exercise can also be performed with your feet together. Focus on keeping your legs and feet off of the ground throughout the entire exercise. This technique provides a tremendous burn for your abdominal muscles, enjoy it!

Exercise

Description

Flutter Kicks

Flutter kicks are excellent for strengthening the lower abs and the upper leg muscles. Place your hands under your buttocks and lift your feet and head about 3 inches off of the ground. Keep one leg straight while raising the opposite leg to approximately 2 feet off of the ground. Maintain strict form by keeping the legs straight and your toes pointed up. Sitting flutter kicks are performed from the sitting position with your hands behind your head. The same flutter kick motion is performed in this variation, but the upper torso is locked in the upright position.

Variation 1

Variation 2

Knee benders and their variations help in stretching and strengthening the abdomin. Whatever variation you choose to perform must be done with strict form and balance. Always remember to keep your legs together and slowly bring them to your chest. These variations are excellent exercises to start your workout with and add a flavor of variety to your routine.

CARDIOVASCULAR – AEROBIC

"Most people seek after what they do not possess and are enslaved by the very things they want to acquire."
-Anwar El-Sadat

Cardiovascular training is one of the most important ingredients to a lifetime of health and happiness. In today's society, it is not uncommon to see men and women in their 80's running and working out. What is the secret or reason that these people use to accomplish this task? Well, there is no secret to it. There is only self-discipline. It takes personal discipline to make yourself get up early, lace up your running shoes and hit the pavement. Cardiovascular exercise dramatically increases your longevity, health, energy, and positive attitude. There is no better way of testing and strengthening your self-discipline than scheduling and sticking to a regular cardio workout.

Regular exercise stimulates the heart and lungs and improves the body's use of oxygen. Exercise can also enhance your skin, muscle tone, breathing, and of course your appearance. These exercises should be:

Regular — repeated three or more times per week.

Vigorous — raising the heart rate to approximately 60-75% of its maximum.

Sustained — performed for at least 30 minutes without interruption.

To produce a cardiovascular training effect, it is important to increase your heart rate to a critical intensity. This intensity is often referred to as the target heart rate. There are many methods and techniques available to monitor all areas of your body's functions during exercise, but this information is of no value to you if you cannot discipline yourself to exercise regularly. The following exercises use large muscle groups, which will help you achieve an overall balanced cardiovascular system.

RUNNING

Jogging and running are commonly used types of aerobic activity. Full body weight is supported and lifted during jogging which is associated with leg injuries. Proper running footwear, surfaces, form, and stretching are key elements to preventing wear and tear on your body. Running allows the individual to open up his mind to clearly focus on his thoughts. It is just as important to have a personal running religion as it is to have one for your calisthenics. By selecting a beautiful, serene, and comfortable running route, you enable the mind to achieve clarity. There is no better way to test your resolve than by running no matter what the conditions or situation. Running is one of the most powerful stress eliminating tools that a person can learn. In the SEAL Teams, we consider running to be an absolute necessity for every aspect of our job. For those people that have a large midsection, it is important to start off with very slow pace.

STAIR/VERSA-CLIMBER

Walking and running stairs have been a very popular method of aerobic exercise, now there are many machines that simulate this great exercise such as the Stairmaster and Versa-Climber. In addition to aerobic development, these machines may also be used to strengthen the upper and lower body. These machines allow the individual to vary the amount of resistance and effort placed upon the body.

CYCLING

Cycling can be a fun and effective form of aerobic conditioning, with the added benefit of reduced muscle trauma. Most stationary cycles provide adjustable workouts and resistance levels. Remember, you get out of it what you put in to it, so focus on maintaining a challenging speed.

WALKING

Walking is becoming one of the most popular growing fitness activities. The impact on the legs is not as great as in running and is excellent for older and obese people. Walking rapidly with hand weights is an excellent way of increasing the cardiovascular output. Keep in mind that as your aerobic capacity increases, you must move on to jogging or running to increase your heart rate and fat burning capacity.

SWIMMING

I hope you didn't think I was going to leave this one out. As you can imagine, swimming is one of the Navy SEAL's favorite and relied upon exercises. The risk of injury to your joints is very low, and can be very beneficial to injury recovery. Swimming, like running, greatly improves the mind's ability to relax and focus on positive thoughts and ideas. Swimming is what I do when I need to focus and work out a problem in my mind.

WARM-UP

It doesn't matter what your age, weight, or fitness level is, your body needs to be properly stretched and warmed up before you begin exercising. Begin by walking for a couple of minutes, followed by slow and focused stretching. Take this time to not only warm up your body, but also your mind. Allow your mind to see positive images and relax to find clarity and motivation.

Walk for a couple of minutes before starting
Always stretch properly
Relax and focus on what is to come
Motivation comes from within, find it

Warm-up Walk:
Walk before you
begin stretching.

Hip Flexor Stretch:
Hold 30 seconds for each leg.

Toe Touches
Hold 30 seconds each leg.

Butterfly Stretch
Groin stretch, hold for
30 seconds.

Knee-Pullers
Quadriceps stretch, hold
for 30 seconds.

Lower Back Stretch
Hold 30 seconds each leg.

COOL-DOWN

Cooling down properly is just as important as warming up. Always take the time to cool down and regain your focus on how your body feels. This is an excellent time to have a notebook in your gym bag to write down any new thoughts or strategies that your mind has worked on. Cooling down both physically and mentally will reduce cramps and your heart rate. If you took the time to practice self-discipline and exercise, don't stop now by forgetting to stretch and cool down. Remember that this is a very powerful time for your mind to think positively and clearly, so focus on your personal improvement and life-goals.

Calf Stretch	**Circles**	**Lateral Stretch**
Hold for 30 seconds each leg.	Do 12 rotations for each arm.	Hold for 30 seconds each side.

 Calm your body, mind, and heart rate to relax.
Onward, walk for another 2 minutes.
Observe caution, repeat stretch routine.
Lean more about your body by relaxing after exercise.

ANATOMY OF THE DISCIPLINED MACHINE

This is the powerful and amazing machine lying underneath all of the unhealthy luggage you have added to your body. Learn and understand all that you can about the major muscle groups and their functions. Form in your mind the image of how your machine looks underneath your fat and skin. Use this image to see what muscles need to be strengthened and toned. Have a distinct picture in your mind's eye of how you want your machine to look and feel. Discipline your mind to test and enhance your machine.

THE MACHINE

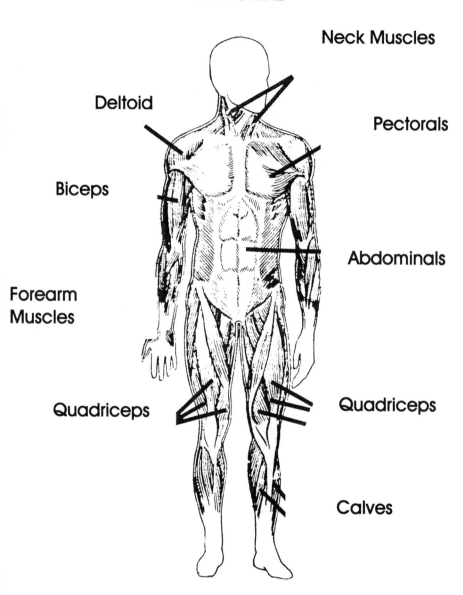

Neck Muscles

Deltoid

Pectorals

Biceps

Abdominals

Forearm
Muscles

Quadriceps

Quadriceps

Calves

THE MACHINE

Trapezius

Triceps

Lower Back Muscles

Latissimus Dorsi

Gluteals

Hamstrings

Calves

"MY BODY HOUSES MY SOUL, TO TAKE CARE OF MY BODY IS TO SOOTHE MY SOUL."
-Samurai Maxim

SEAL TEAM RUNNING TECHNIQUES

"Be not afraid of greatness: some are born great, some achieve greatness, and some have greatness thrust upon them."
-William Shakespeare

In the SEAL Teams running is a way of life and not just a form of exercise. Running provides daily obstacles and tests that challenge our self-discipline and fitness level. By reaching deep inside and finding the will to run no matter what the weather or time of day, provides a powerful dose of clarity. In order to receive all of the wonderful benefits of a running routine, you must first learn and understand how to run correctly. Use the information that is provided here, culled from years of special operations running experience to provide a solid foundation for your personal running program.

Warm-Up

A warm-up to stretch tight muscles before running is crucial for preventing injuries that can result from tight and cold muscles. A stretched and longer muscle is less likely to get injured than a short, tight muscle. Warming up helps protect the legs by stimulating your tendons. Warm up slowly by walking or jogging for five minutes prior to beginning your stretch routine.

Running Form

Running is a function of footstrike, body angle, and arm drive. The key to having proper running form is to run relaxed and move naturally.

Stride

The point of foot contact should be in line with the knee, which should be slightly flexed. As your fitness level improves and you get faster, the length of your stride will increase and you will begin lifting your knees higher. Concentrate on not overstriding when you run (i.e. foot hits the ground in front of knee flex). Overstriding is very hard on the knees and tendons and can cause injuries. Choppy, short strides usually result from inflexible or tight muscles and are very inefficient. Run with a comfortable and relaxed stride, but do not over exaggerate your leg movements.

Footstrike

Unless you are a sprinter or competitive runner, the heel-ball footstrike method is for you: (1) the outside of the heel strikes the surface; (2) the foot rolls inwards to the ball of the foot while the knee is slightly bent; and (3) the foot is pushed off of the ground by the big toe. This technique provides maximum efficiency and excellent shock absorption.

Body Angle

The trick to maintaining proper body angle is to keep your back as straight as comfortably possible, your head up and looking ahead. Sometimes, depending upon the terrain, you will have to look down to navigate over and around obstacles. Lean forward only when going uphill as this position puts stress on your leg muscles. Do not lean back, as this will put unwanted pressure on your back and act as a "brake". The trick is to run relaxed and tall; allow your shoulders to relax and shake your arms out from time to time.

Arm Motion

Allow your elbows, upper arms, wrists, and hands to occasionally relax and hang down at your sides. Fast and tight pumping of the arms is very inefficient and unnecessary for relaxed running.

Running Frequency

Schedule your runs for at least three or four times per week or every other day. It is important to schedule several rest days in your weekly exercise program. A rest day is not necessarily a no exercise day, but rather a day of an alternate type of exercise. This allows your running muscles to recover and repair.

Intensity and Speed

You should run at a comfortable and relaxed pace that allows you to talk and think. If you run too fast and furious, you will expend all of your energy in a short amount of time. Running fast tends to tighten muscles and must be followed by a long cool-down stretching period. Speed is not as important as distance and time.

8 Tricks of the Trade

1. Do not overstride.
2. Relax and think.
3. Run tall.
4. Run naturally.
5. Pick a pleasant area and route.
6. Purchase the proper shoes and clothing.
7. Hydrate, hydrate, and hydrate some more.
8. Stretch before and after your run.

MISSION #4

"When we walk to the edge of all the light we have and take the step into the darkness of the unknown, we must believe that one of two things will happen. There will be something solid for us to stand on or we will be taught to fly."
-Patrick Overton

This mission is designed to be the first step that you will take towards mastering physical discipline. I have given you a great deal of information and many techniques that will provide a solid foundation from which to build upon. However, the one thing that I cannot do is force you to get out there and do it. You must make the decision here and now, to take control of your body and its maintenance. Life is about decisions and actions; this minute, this hour, is one of those times to decide and act. I want you to relax and focus on your thoughts on what areas of your body need conditioning and improvement. In your mind's eye formulate a picture of "your machine" underneath your skin and visualize the areas that you would like to enhance.

The type of exercise that you decide to undertake in the beginning is not as important as actually finding the discipline to adhere to a routine. You must develop a daily exercise schedule and begin taking the steps to achieving what you have written down. In the next couple of days, I want you to list your favorite physical activities in a personal exercise journal and start implementing them into your exercise schedule. You do not need to plan for a whole month's worth of exercise at first, but rather one day or one week at a time. Remember that it is the small victories that provide us with the power to take on the large battles in our quest for life-mastery.

CHAPTER 5 - NUTRITIONAL WARFARE

*"Twenty years from now you will be more disappointed by the
things you didn't do than by the ones you did do. So throw off
the bowlines. Sail away from the safe harbor. Catch the trade
winds in your sails. Explore. Dream. Discover."*

-Mark Twain

You are what you eat. By changing your diet, you can
dramatically enhance your body, mind, emotions, moods, energy levels,
and longevity. All of the information and techniques found in this book
are of no value if you do not have the health and energy to begin utilizing
and applying them to your life. This chapter is about the fuel we put into
our machines and how it effects our lives. By caring for your body with
proper and disciplined nutrition, you will have the power and vitality
needed to achieve your life goals. In Far-East societies, what a person
eats is thought to be directly related to his or her mental intelligence and
physical toughness. Fruits and vegetables, along with a meat-less diet are

responsible for providing a powerful flow of energy and personal enlightenment.

Today, many scientific studies now conclude that the body and mind are powerfully connected and if one is not operating at peak levels, the other suffers drastically. Begin treating and maintaining both of these precious miracles with careful nutrition and create the powerful life you deserve. Make no mistake about it, eating properly is a constant battle that hangs your life in the balance. Nutritional warfare is a concept of techniques and information that will provide you with the ability to successfully do battle with the forces of evil that lurk in our stores, restaurants, and refrigerators every day.

What element exists that enables a person to choose the proper food over desired food? That element is self-discipline! The powers of the mind and body are joined to focus our thoughts and actions in to a predetermined response. The response we are looking for is one of proper selection and decision making when you open your mouth to ingest selected body fuel.

In order to gain control over the mental and physical action of eating, we must first understand how the process works. We are preprogrammed to respond in a certain way to the sounds, smells, and tastes of certain foods. The program that exists in our brain is the result of our memories, ancestors, chemical reactions, and trends of society. In nature, there are predators and gatherers of food. The lion is a meat-eating predator and the monkey is a gatherer of fruits and vegetables. The grizzly bear is a predator and the gorilla is a gatherer of vegetation and fruits. This is not to say that predators always eat meat and gatherers always eat fruit and vegetables, but that one is designed for a different lifestyle than the other. As a human being, do you have extended carnivorous teeth, deadly claws, or the ability to run down and kill for meat? No, but you do have flexible hands and an opposing thumb, the ability to grow food, and the physical characteristics of a food gatherer. I am not saying that you must give up meat all together, rather that like most gatherers our diet must consist of 90% fruits, grains, and vegetables. When you do eat meat for protein, make it lean chicken, fish, or turkey instead of red meat in any form.

The ancient people of the Himalayas are a perfect study on mental clarity, physical strength, and longevity. Many live well beyond 100 and maintain sharp minds and strong bodies throughout their lives, performing incredible feats well past our society's retirement age. These self-disciplined masters go for weeks on end without food or sleep and can endure very high levels of pain in adverse conditions. What is the secret of their powerful lives? It is simply that they eat in moderation and follow a strict natural diet with self-discipline.

The 5,000-year-old diet that the Himalayan people follow is a pure diet based on living foods – those created by nature, sun, air, water, and Mother Earth. The disciplined diet focuses on fruits, fruit juices, vegetables, grains, and white meats. By making changes to your diet that ensure these life-giving foods make up at least 85% of your intake, you will win the first important battle of nutritional warfare. In order to gain physical mastery and life-control, you must dig deep inside yourself and find the will to eat natural and fresh foods only. Meat products are simply dead foods. Our stomach and intestines are dramatically different than carnivores and are more anatomically similar to fruit and vegetation-eating primates. Animal flesh has been found to have high proportions of chemicals and toxins. Dead meat also lacks most of the important vitamins and minerals that we need to function at peak levels, and is also very hard to digest because of the large amount of energy required to break it down. Have you ever noticed how slow, sluggish, and lethargic you feel after eating a big steak? Compare this to how you feel after eating a large and healthy salad that is easily digested.

141

If meat is so hard on our bodies, why do we eat it? Many people argue that vegetarian diets do not provide proper protein, but ironically those who eat a lot of meat ingest the lowest quality protein available. Meat contains a high concentration of uric acid, which cannot be broken down by the liver and can lead to deadly health problems. Fruits, vegetables, and certain dairy products provide a superior quality of protein than that found in meat. Take a look at the most powerful animals on this planet; the gorilla and the elephant have about 35 times the strength of a human and subsist completely on fruits, grains, and vegetables.

THE COMMANDO DIET

"Everyone thinks of changing the world, but no one thinks of changing himself."
-Leo Tolstoy

At the very heart of the commando diet are fresh fruit and vegetables. Our bodies are at least 70% water; since fruits and vegetables also are very high in water, they are most perfectly suited to our body composition. The water contained in fruits and vegetables is important for energy and cleansing. Water carries the cargo of nutrients into our intestines, where they are quickly absorbed. The water then carries away the waste. One of the most important concepts of using fruits and vegetables is to select organic produce only. By selecting organic produce, you eliminate the influx of pesticides, toxins, and chemicals that are introduced into your body from commercially grown produce.

To get the most out of your produce, I highly recommend that you eat most of it raw as cooking depletes their nutritional value. If you are going to cook it, it is important that you cook produce for only a couple of minutes. Vegetables need not to be eaten plain to be healthy. A highly nutritious and tasteful way of preparing vegetables is to make a meat-less stew. The broth of the cooked vegetables is very high in nutrients and minerals. A vegetable broth not only energizes your body, but also greatly assists in cleansing your body of its stored toxins.

Another source of powerful nutrients and minerals are water vegetables. Edible seaweeds have long been a regular part of the diet of coastal peoples such as the Pacific Islanders, the Japanese, and the Irish. Sea vegetables are extremely rich in iodine and other minerals, and are a very important food for healthy skin, hair, nails, bones, and teeth. The iodine in sea vegetables stimulates the thyroid gland, and ensures proper metabolism and a healthy reproductive system.

POWER FOODS

Some foods provide such a powerful combination of nutrition, taste, and health benefits that they deserve to be classified as power foods. These foods are so life-enhancing that some ancient religions thought that they were given to them by the gods. The healthiest and longest living societies make these foods the foundation of their diets.

SPROUTS

Sprouted seeds, whole grains, and legumes are among the most powerful and healthiest foods on this planet. They are a perfect example of living foods that carries nutrients directly to your body's most basic cells. Sprouts are extremely high in the purest forms of protein, enzymes, and lecithin. The rich enzymes in sprouts trigger your digestive system to power-up and cleanse itself. Sprouts contain minerals and vitamins that are extremely low in calories. Sprouts encompass a group of seeds, legumes, and whole grains that include rye, yellow soy, wheat, sunflower, radish, lentils and radishes.

LECITHIN

This power food comes from soybeans and can be purchased as a supplement in granular form at most health food stores. Lecithin flushes fat from the liver and prevents it from collecting in the bloodstream. When digested, lecithin produces acetylcholine, which removes lactic acid from the body, muscles, and joints to provide a healthier and more flexible body. Lecithin also helps flush away toxins and waste from the nerve cells and helps enhance the reflexes.

GARLIC

Garlic is very high in selenium, a powerful anti-aging nutrient that has been proven to control heart disease, intestinal problems, high blood pressure, liver diseases, and sinus conditions. Garlic is also extremely efficient at reducing triglyceride and cholesterol levels in the blood. A study of people over one hundred years old found that the only practice they shared in common was that they consumed large quantities of garlic. This powerful food is one of the cornerstones to life-extension and vitality.

WHOLE GRAINS

Unprocessed grains contain important nutrients like vitamin E, vitamin B, and bran fiber, that help in cleaning the walls of your intestines. Several types of grains are considered to be complete protein food in addition to supplying the body with powerful nutrients and minerals. Grains such as Barley, Millet, and Buckwheat are the foundation of life-enhancing diets that have been in existence for thousands of years.

ONIONS

This plant belongs to the same family as garlic, and like garlic, helps bring cholesterol levels down and prevents the clumping of platelets. This vegetable, especially if eaten raw, help to prevent the gathering of unwanted fats in the arteries that can lead to heart attacks and strokes. Onions also help in killing harmful bacteria without hurting your body's naturally friendly bacteria.

HERBS

Natural herbs have been used to heal any ailment, prevent injuries, increase memory and intelligence, and greatly extend a person's life since recorded history. For some reason, with our advanced and intellectual society of today, we instead consume chemicals, toxins, pesticides, artificial foods, deadly fats, and life-reducing foods on a regular basis. There are hundreds of herbs and various combinations that extremely enhance the quality and productivity of your life.

The commando diet is designed to offer a realistic, intelligent, and life-extending system of foods that you can use to enhance the quality of your life. By incorporating fruits, vegetables, grains, power foods, supplements, proteins and self-discipline, the commando diet turns food into a weapon instead of a detriment.

PROTEIN FOODS

Most scientific studies have shown that Americans eat much more protein than their bodies require. An over-load of protein in the diet generates toxic nitrogen by-products that over burden the kidneys. Studies also have concluded that societies that eat high animal-protein diets have a much higher rate of cancer. With the commando diet, you will notice a lighter feeling and an overall improvement in your digestion.

If you are going to eat animal flesh protein, stick to chicken and fish prepared by grilling, broiling, or steaming. Another option for your protein intake is soy, tofu, and supplemental protein drinks. As you select your protein meals, try a different source of protein every day to reduce the stress on your digestive system.

Dairy foods must be reduced or eliminated completely. Many people have a hard time digesting milk, while cheese congests the system and dehydrates the body through constipation. Cheese should be considered as an infrequent high-fat treat, not a dietary staple to your diet. Yogurt is easier to assimilate than any other dairy product, but still requires considerable energy to digest. There are many different sources of calcium besides dairy products, including leafy greens, sesame seeds, raw nuts, corn tortillas, broccoli, and sea vegetables. I strongly recommend calcium supplements for most people, no matter what foods they eat.

FATS

Many people are under the impression that if you want to lose weight and prevent heart disease, you cannot eat fat at all. The truth is that there are some good fats that are essential to healthy living. To enhance your health, increase vitality, and flush the fat out of your body, you need a daily supply of good fats. Good fats are known as Omega-6 and Omega-3 oils, or GLAs and EPAs. Many people come to me for help after years of starving their bodies on low-fat, low-calorie diets. They complain of dry skin and hair, constipation, and weak and brittle nails. By adding the essential EPA and EPA oils to their diet, these problems are reversed. It is the EPAs, or Omega-3 oils, in the diet of the Eskimos that prevent them from having heart disease, despite a heavy diet of animal fat and protein. Many societies that eat large quantities of fish have a very low incidence of heart disease, confirming the powerful effects of EPA.

Omega-6 oils are even more important than the EPAs for protecting the cardiovascular system, heart, immune system, and the skin. These powerful oils flush the fat out of the body, and when both Omega-3 and Omega-6 are combined together, the health benefits are unmatched. Some unrefined vegetable oils such as safflower, borage, evening-primrose, corn, soy and sesame oil all provide high levels of GLAs for your body. Recent research has shown that olive oil can dramatically reduce the levels of LDL, the dangerous blood cholesterol, while keeping HDL, the beneficial form, intact. This fact could be the reason why the Mediterranean peoples such as Italians and Greeks, who use large amounts of olive oil, have half the death rate from heart disease than do Americans. Olive oil carries mono unsaturated fats, as do nuts and avocados. Canola oil has recently been found to contain large amounts of mono-unsaturated fats as well, and can be used in light cooking. It is important to understand that reducing your intake of all types of fat is healthy, but if you are going to consume any fats, make them the good ones.

SUPPLEMENTS

In today's society, supplements are looked at as the quick fix to all personal health problems. The problem with our diet is that we eat large amounts of very unhealthy foods and wonder why we are overweight, tired, mentally drained, and ill. Most Americans think that if they take some supplements after eating two Big Macs and fries, that this will make everything better. There are so many different types of supplements out on the market today, that it would take a whole book to just cover 10% of them. If you make a disciplined decision to find out all that you can about various supplements and how they can help or hamper your personal commando diet, you will have taken another step in winning the nutritional war. I am a strong believer of supplementation, and daily use supplements to enhance my performance, health, and longevity. For simplicity sake, I have grouped nutritional supplements, ergogenic agents, and herbs together in hopes of reducing confusion. Below I have listed some of the supplements that can have dramatic effects upon your health and performance.

Vitamin A, B, C, and E

Calcium and Selenium

Goldenseal

Saw Palmetto Berry

Ginkgo Biloba

St John's Wort

Coenzyme Q10

Chromium

Branch-Chain Amino Acids

Garlic

Omega-3 & Omega-6 oils

DHEA

Fresh Squeezed Juices

Antioxidants

Aspirin

Wheat Germ Oil

Ginseng & Green Tea

Zinc & Magnesium

Glucosamine Sulfate

Wheatgrass Juice

Yohimbe

Carnitine

Potassium

Echinacea

Niacin

Ephedra (selective use)

Bilberry Extract

Creatine Monohydrate

Guarana

Whey Protein

Recent studies have shown that by taking adequate levels of vitamin E, Vitamin C, magnesium, and selenium the rate of heart disease could be reduced by up to 50 percent. This alone could result in over $50 billion in health care savings per year. This represents savings from just one health problem. Any way you look at it, taking vitamin-herb-mineral supplementation is going to reduce your healthcare costs and enhance your longevity. Take the time to educate yourself on the world of supplements, vitamins, herbs, and minerals. You must begin your personal commando diet by re-programming the way you eat, and what you eat. You must take a war-like approach to nutrition and diet.

A lot of people tell me that they would start taking supplements if they were not so darn expensive, but if you look at what they actually spend money on in the grocery store, you would see just how ridiculous this statement is. According to *The 1992 Top-Ten Almanac* by Michael Robbins (Workman Publishing), the top ten items purchased in our grocery stores, ranked by dollar volume, are:

1.   Marlboro cigarettes
2.   Coca Cola Classic
3.   Pepsi Cola
4.   Kraft Processed Cheese
5.   Diet Coke
6.   Campbell's Soup
7.   Budweiser beer
8.   Tide detergent
9.   Folger's coffee
10. Winston cigarettes

Do you wonder why you are fat and sick? Does your body run on cigarettes and beer? Did you know that most of these items are consumed while watching television? It is amazing to me that we can put a man on the moon, but we cannot find the discipline to stop killing ourselves! If societies 5,000 years ago found the secrets to a lifetime of health, happiness, and vitality, just how far advanced is our society? The message is written out in black and white for all of us to see, but what is it that we lack to put this information into action. What we as a society are lacking, is simply self-discipline and commitment. Nutritional warfare has become a battle for each and every one of us, due to the fact that everywhere we shop, look, and eat we are bombarded with deadly foods, toxins, chemicals, and false information. This is the battle that you must begin fighting today.

It is true that many people in the United States tend to gain weight with age, but it is not necessary that we do. Getting fatter as we get older is not without increased health risks. Diseases associated with aging such as heart disease, stroke, and diabetes are more prevalent in overweight people. Metabolism slows about 5 percent every decade after 30, therefore we have to decrease our food intake by that much just to stay at our present weight. We tend to lose muscle and bone with age as well. We can slow down the effects of declining muscle mass and metabolism if we eat right and remain physically active. Muscle tissue is more metabolically active than fat, therefore metabolism increases with an increase in muscle mass.

Since less than 10 percent of the United States population currently exercises regularly three times per week, it is easy to see why most people believe it is normal to gain weight with age. There are four crucial components needed to lose weight effectively and forever.

FOUR COMPONENTS OF WEIGHT LOSS

1. Regular aerobic and strength enhancing exercise.
2. A living foods, low-fat, high fiber, and supplemented diet.
3. Moderate calorie restriction.
4. Disciplined lifestyle change that incorporates these three factors.

Many people choose to do only one of these components. They initially may lose weight, but at some point the weight loss stops and they get bigger than they were before. The word "diet" implies that you are going on or coming off of something. A diet also implies that you are restricted from doing something, which usually leaves you feeling deprived. For this reason, most people who are on diets always fail at keeping the weight off. A healthy living foods diet and regular exercise is a lifestyle change that will lead to a powerful, beautiful, efficient, and long living body filled with vitality. By using the power-living concept of personal management, we discipline ourselves to become aware of our daily intake of food. Through mastering self-discipline, your food and exercise patterns become clearer as you write them down.

Here are ten questions you must find answers to:

1. How many calories do I really eat?
2. How much bad fat do I really eat?
3. Do I skip meals?
4. How many servings of fruits and vegetables do I eat?
5. Do I eat when I am stressed out or upset?
6. When is my first meal of the day?
7. What portion sizes am I eating?
8. How much time and effort do I spend planning my food intake?
9. How often do I prepare my own meals?
10. How much time do I spend learning about food and nutrition?

Water is the most basic element of life. Without water, death occurs within days. Your body is approximately 40-65% water. Water is essential for the process of absorption and digestion of nutrients, and excretion of bodily wastes. Water plays a significant role in the regulation of body temperature and mental awareness. There is nothing special with regards to weight loss and water drinking. Drinking water will not flush fat out of your body, but it will keep you well hydrated. By increasing your water intake at mealtime, you will reduce the urge to overeat. Water is supplied from both food and liquids.

A diet high in organic fruits and vegetables goes a long way in keeping your body hydrated. There is no provision for water storage in the human body; therefore, we must replace the amount lost every 24 hours to maintain optimal health. Normally, about 2.5 liters of water (ten 8-ounce cups) are required each day for a sedentary adult in a normal environment.

NUTRITIONAL WARFARE BASICS

"The building of a perfect body crowned by a perfect brain, is at once the greatest earthly problem and grandest hope of the race."
-Dio Lewis

Nutrition is the science of nourishment, and the study of nutrients and the processes by which organisms utilize them. Nutritional warfare is based on the powerful concepts and principals that have been established for over 5,000 years. Poor nutritional warfare decision-making can mean the difference between life and death. All living organisms need proper nutrition to function and live normally. Here are the six nutrients found in foods.

The Six Nutrients in Food

1. Protein
2. Fats
3. Carbohydrates
4. Minerals
5. Vitamins
6. Water

Proteins, carbohydrates, and fat provide the body with calories. Vitamins, water, and minerals provide no calories for your body. Carbohydrates and proteins supply the body with four calories per weight gram, and fats supply the body with nine calories per gram. Carbohydrates are starches and sugars in food that are usually called simple and complex carbohydrates. They provide the main fuel and energy source in the body. Examples of complex carbohydrates include bread, pasta, rice, cereals, and whole grain foods. Simple carbohydrates include fruits and vegetables. Refined simple sugars include table sugar, which is found in processed foods like cookies, candy, cakes, sodas, fruit punch, and ice cream.

Protein is made up of amino acids that are broken down during the digestion process. Amino acids are often referred to as the "building blocks" of protein. Protein is vital to the human body as it functions to repair and build tissue, as well as develop the formation of hormones, antibodies, and enzymes. Amino acids are classified as either nonessential or essential. Amino acids that can be produced in the body are called nonessential and the eight amino acids that the body cannot produce are called essential. They must be provided by the food in our diet. Complete proteins are foods that contain large amounts of essential amino acids. Some forms of complete protein are foods such as chicken, fish, eggs, and milk. Proteins that cannot supply the body with all of the essential amino acids are known as incomplete proteins. These come from non-animal sources such as legumes, grains, and vegetables. By combining two incomplete proteins, a complete protein can be obtained, if all essential amino acids are provided by the food combination. This is the heart of the commando diet system. When we eliminate unhealthy red meats and dairy products from our diets, we must choose alternate forms of protein to supplement this loss.

The commando diet stresses living foods and thoughtful supplementation of vitamins, proteins, minerals, and herbs. Since each human being is different, it is up to you to find the proper combinations and amounts that work best for your body.

COMMANDO DIET ESSENTIALS

"You wake up in the morning, and your purse is magically filled with twenty-four hours of unmanufactured tissue of the universe of your life! It is yours. It is the most precious of possessions. No one can take it from you. And no one receives either more or less than you receive."
-Dr. Thomas Arnold Bennett

Energy is the first essential element of power living, for without an abundance of it you are like a car without gas. For optimal energy, it is important that you eat according to the natural cycles that occur in your body. They are as follows:

1. **The Feeding Cycle** 12 p.m. – 8 p.m. (Power foods such as fruits and vegetables ingested and digested.)

2. **The Absorption Cycle** 8 p.m.– 4 a.m. (The foods are expended.)

3. **The Removal Cycle** 4 a.m. – 12 p.m (The foods are excreted.)

By understanding these natural cycles and eating foods that allow these cycles to operate effectively, you will tap into your powerful energy reserves and see a tremendous increase in overall health. By flushing the toxins out of the body, we ensure that it remains pure inside. By practicing the commando power living dict, we allow our bodies to repair and flush themselves of harmful toxins in a natural way. The process of flushing out our bodies is accomplished in the following way:

1. Eating greater amounts of high-water content foods.

Your body composition is approximately 65% water, so to properly cleanse your body and ensure that it is operating at peak levels, your diet must consist of at least 65% water content. By eating plenty of fruits and vegetables and drinking plenty of water, we are able to maintain this peak performance range.

2. Understanding the body's three cycles.

Now that we have begun to eat high-water content power foods, we must ensure that your eating cycles are scheduled into our body's three functioning cycles. Begin by eating only fruits and vegetables for breakfast, as the body is now trying to get rid of unwanted wastes and toxins. This allows the elimination and excretion process to operate at peak efficiency. During mid-day, have your proteins, grains, fruits, supplements, and vegetables. You should not ingest any foods after 8:30 p.m., as this will greatly effect your absorption cycle by overworking your digestive system. This technique will powerfully enhance the quality of your sleep.

These essential elements of the power living commando diet are not as difficult to follow as it first may seem. In the morning when your body is eliminating toxins and waste, start off the day with several bananas, oranges, apples, or a glass of fruit juice. By utilizing self-discipline techniques, you will automatically reach for the fruits and juices instead of eggs, bacon, toast, and coffee. For lunch and dinner, make sure your meals are full of fresh grains and vegetables to ensure peak energy and health levels are maintained throughout the rest of the day. The results you will experience from the power living commando diet will be noticed on the very first day. This system is not some "magical" diet, or insane new age lifestyle, simply the natural flow of energy, life, and vitality. Your health, mental state, and energy levels will increase to levels that you have never experienced before.

In order to conserve essential energy for your day, it is important that you understand the concept of controlled digestion. If you are like most people, gobbling down your lunch while watching television or taking care of work-related business is a daily occurrence. Proper and controlled chewing of all food might sound like a simple task but it is extremely essential for power living and vitality. The saliva that is concentrated in your mouth is designed to initially break down the food that you eat. Large chunks of undigested food are tremendously stressful on your stomach's digestive system, requiring large amounts of energy to break down. How often do you feel tired and lethargic after eating a quick lunch or dinner? How many times a week do you feel like taking a noontime nap? If you are like most Americans, the answer to these questions is most likely – every day!

Properly chewed food is digested much easier, which also means your body needs less of it. The body will require less food intake when you slowly and thoughtfully chew your food. In today's society, people eat much more food than they actually need which in turn becomes converted to fat. By simply taking an extra 10 to 15 seconds to chew your food, the benefits of greater energy and a leaner body will be added to your life. Think of your digestive system as the engine to your machine. Just like your vehicle's engine, proper fuel and maintenance is directly related to its life span and performance.

MISSION #5

"You cannot run away from a weakness; you must sometimes fight it out or perish. And if that be so, why not now, and where you stand?"
-Robert Louis Stevenson

Now that you understand the basics of the commando diet, we must begin to implement its powerful concepts into your life. In the SEAL Teams, we must be able to effectively operate in all environmental extremes. In one week, we could find ourselves in the searing heat of the African dessert and the next week in the sub-freezing cold of the Arctic. In order to effectively prepare our bodies for such extremes, we use a technique called acclimatization. By preparing our minds and bodies with the needed information, equipment, clothing, and food, we are better able to understand and combat the dramatic effects of rapid change. It is through the process of understanding how and why our bodies react to various food changes, temperatures, and conditions that we are able to predict and counteract the stresses of change.

For this mission we are going to begin the process of acclimatizing to a new country or environment. The only foods to be found in this new country are fruits, vegetables, supplements, grains, chicken, and fish. This foreign country has no McDonalds, 7-11's, Pizza Huts, or restaurants of any kind. In order to prepare yourself for this upcoming mission, you must slowly start adapting to this food change by altering your present diet. To successfully accomplish this mission, you must begin studying, understanding, and consuming these new foods. Each day we will begin eating less of our regular foods and more of these new foods, until we have successfully adapted to this country's indigenous diet.

It is important to understand that just eating these foods is not enough, you must begin researching and studying all that you can about the relationship between your body and these foods. By keeping a daily journal of what, where, why, and how you eat these foods, we are better able to understand the effects of these new foods on our bodies.

The powerful effects of the commando diet upon your body will truly amaze you. By the end of the week you will feel a tremendous vibrancy and energy like you have never felt before. The benefits of eating living foods and eliminating dead, processed foods from your diet will make you a true believer. The path to power living must begin with self-discipline. All of the information that you have just read is worthless unless you begin disciplining yourself to take action today. You are a big person now, so start taking responsibility for your body and its care. You are what you eat.

MISSION DEBRIEF

"It is better to conquer yourself than to win a thousand battles. Then the victory is yours. It cannot be taken from you, not by angels or by demons, heaven or hell."
- Buddha

The powerful effects that you are feeling from the commando diet are a direct result of self-disciplined eating. The concept of nutritional warfare is one of knowledge and action. By ensuring that we eat only living and unprocessed foods, we tremendously enhance our health, clarity, energy, and vitality. How do you expect to be successful in life if you can't even control how and what you eat? The introduction of self-discipline into our eating habits is a sometimes difficult and demanding task. By utilizing the techniques of visualization and thought control, we can program our minds to erase urges and impulses. The most powerful weapon in the war of nutrition is information. It is up to you to develop the foundation of knowledge needed to properly select and purchase living foods. You can read all of the personal empowerment books that you want, but it is ultimately self-discipline that makes your actions speak louder than words.

Why keep polluting your body with toxins and chemicals when you now know better? Who is going to hold your hand when you go food shopping or out to a restaurant? Who is responsible for the body in the mirror that you so dislike? What don't you have the energy to accomplish certain tasks, or to think and reason with clarity? The answers to these questions are right in front of us every day, but sometimes we need a little reminder or motivator to smack us alongside the head and say, "Hey dummy, quit killing yourself!" If you continue to overeat dead and processed foods, you will succeed in killing yourself sooner or later. By adding self-discipline to our eating habits, we begin the transition from dying to power living.

It is very important to keep a daily journal of all the information pertaining to our eating habits. Everybody has a bad day and makes a few poor decisions, but through self-discipline and personal management we are able to dramatically reduce the occurrence of these glitches. I am a firm believer in treating yourself to whatever you want every now and then, but that does not apply to every day! By giving in a little every day, you are only treating yourself to illness, obesity, low self-esteem, and death. It is not so hard, stand up and take responsibility for your actions and life. Start getting everything you want out of life by making a commitment. By adding a little of self-discipline into your life, you begin reaping the tremendous benefits of power living. Health, vitality, success, beauty, and longevity are yours for the taking; all that you need is commitment and self-discipline.

CHAPTER 6 - THE PREDATOR'S MINDSET

"There are things known, and there are things unknown. And in between are the doors of perception."

-Jim Morrison

About 2,500 years ago, a Greek physician by the name of Hippocrates stated, "Men ought to know that from the brain – and from the brain only, arise our pleasures, laughters, and successes – as well as our sorrows, pains, griefs, and failures." I often wonder how mentally advanced and how different our world would be if the human race had followed the advice and teachings of ancient wisdom. Imagine how advanced our technology and mental powers would be if we had followed the advice of ancient scholars and used our brains to reprogram ourselves for health, wealth, control, and happiness. I wonder if we would be able to control our bodily functions like the Shoalin and Tibetan monks of the Himalayas, or would have developed the powers of clairvoyance and ESP. I can only imagine how many wars and conflicts would have been avoided if we had continued to learn about the amazing powers of our minds.

The ability to have everything you have ever desired, great wealth, love, peace, fame and success, health and prosperity, has been in your head since you took your first breath of air. Infinite riches are yours for the taking, if you will open your mind to become a predator instead of a lamb.

The problem lies in the fact that most people are in the realm of the walking dead, because they don't know about the gold mine of infinite intelligence and boundless ability within them. Whatever you want out of life you can have, but you must develop the mindset of success, self-discipline, and domination. In life there are two types of people, those who continually dominate their environment and those who are dominated by their environment. The predator sits on top of the human food chain and knows that he or she is born to dominate and succeed. Then there is the lamb, the average human, who is full of fears, doubts, and negative thoughts. Opportunities come, and they say, " I can't" or "I might fail" or "I might lose my money" or "I am just unlucky". This type of person will never get past the average existence, they will remain in a stagnate cycle of average performance and living. The age of television and computers has disabled the basic human traits of self-control, persistence, and domination. Today, the average American spends four hours out of each day staring at a television. We have effectively removed ourselves from the hunt for success by mesmerizing our minds with television

The secret to rediscovering the predator mindset is found in your mind, the last place most people would think to look. Through the process of suggestion, self-talk, and mental discipline, you can bring into your life more power, wealth, health, happiness, and satisfaction than you can imagine. In order to establish the predator mindset, you need to develop the attitude of domination, persistence, and focused discipline in the direction of your goals. The predator mindset is about pushing past your perceived limitations by disciplining your thoughts and actions to ensure they are focused on achieving your goals. Instead of sitting in front of the television for several hours each day, dedicate this time to working on starting your own business, exercising, reading, learning a new skill, or working on self-improvement. The predator mindset is about accepting challenges, taking calculated risks, overcoming fears, and breaking free from the chains of the average lifestyle.

The predator mindset is not an aggressive attitude toward your fellow man, but rather an aggressive attitude towards achieving all that you desire. It is an attitude of thinking and acting in a manner that is above average. It is about doing things that average people are unwilling to do. If the average human spends his evening watching television, eating junk food, and complaining about the way things are, then above average performance requires spending your evening working towards your goals, eating a healthy meal, and discovering ways to change things for the better. This is the basis behind the predator mindset and the foundation of success and personal achievement. In order to begin developing this focused mental and physical energy, we must tap into the limitless power of our minds.

The human mind can be programmed for success, discipline, and achievement with the tool of self-talk. Self-talk is a method of directly programming the subconscious mind with the attitude and information necessary for success. Self-talk is a very powerful programming technique. Self-talk is a dynamic method of thought control through which thoughts, ideas, plans, and actions are placed in the conscious mind, and through repetition become ingrained into the subconscious mind. Here these concepts are picked up and carried out to their logical conclusion. The transfer of thought from self-talk to the subconscious mind can be quickened and enforced by the power of faith, fear, or any other highly intensified emotion, such as enthusiasm and the burning desire to attain a goal. Thoughts backed by faith have precedence over all others, because they are more powerful and are carried out quicker. The speed with which these thoughts are brought into reality when backed by faith, gives rise to the belief held by many that certain phenomena are the result of miracles.

It is a known fact, that a person who is capable of freeing his or her mind from all self-imposed limitations, through the technique of self-talk and faith, generally finds the solution to all existing problems, regardless of their nature. Self-talk is the power behind a positive mental attitude, and gives life to the feelings and thoughts of happiness. It is a profound truth of nature, that whatever you impress upon the subconscious mind through self-talk, will eventually manifest itself into a present reality. If you continually fill your mind with thoughts of failure, depression, weakness, poverty, and limitation, you will experience these in reality. However, if you fill your mind with thoughts of success, domination, achievement, and possibility, you will rise above the average human sheep herd to become a predator of success.

Successful people became successful only because they have acquired the habit of thinking like a predator, rather than a lamb. The majority of their thoughts are centered around the belief that they can and will attain what they desire. When a negative thought enters the mind, it must be quickly replaced with a positive thought through self-talk. The power of subconscious thought is 100 times more powerful than conscious thought. The great philosophers throughout time, from Plato and Socrates to Emerson and Ghandi, are all known to have used self-talk in programming themselves for achievement.

One of the most important aspects of the predator mindset, is the determination of your desires. You must take the time to ask yourself what it is that you really want from life. Every human alive will tell you that they would like to have lots of money, happiness, respect, love, and success. Take the time to be very specific on your ultimate goals in each of these areas.

The attitude of domination and achievement, the predator mindset, produces actions of domination and achievement, but remember that faith determines how quickly your subconscious mind begins to work on these realities. One of the reasons that the predator mindset has been so powerful and successful in my life is because of my faith in God. The predator mindset is about breaking down our self-imposed limitations. If you feel tired and lethargic, break your comfort zone by staying up all night to work on your goals. If you are afraid to speak in public, stand up in front of the largest crowd you can find and give it a try. If you have dreams of working for yourself, take a calculated risk, make a plan, and quit your job. Remember that sheep are held prisoner by a wooden fence, but you are held prisoner only by a mental fence.

Human beings are creatures of habit. We create routines in our lives to give us a feeling of security and control. Routines become a protective mechanism against the uncertainty and constant change of everyday life. Being creatures of habit, we function more efficiently in an organized and controlled system of activities. We thrive on having consistent schedules, time-lines, eating habits, and social interactions that form our daily routines. In order to minimize the effects of change and uncertainty in our lives, we build routines to give us a sense of control.

Routines are like fences that we build up in our lives to create a comfort zone against the effects of change. We become comfortable knowing how, when, where, and what we are going to be doing from day to day. In order to realize our potential, we must begin to grow and make forward progress in the direction of our goals and this can only come about through change. Achieving anything of value requires risk, vision, and hard work, but none of these attributes can flourish in a comfort zone. You must break free from your comfort zone to begin discovering the predator of success and achievement sleeping inside of you.

One of the most powerful methods for awakening the predator inside, is to fill your mind with the thoughts, ideas, and wisdom of the world's most successful people. Throughout history, successful and dominating people have left behind the secrets to their lifelong achievements. Every action and thought that is directed toward your goals, must be part of a well thought-out plan. The quickest way to develop the momentum of success is to learn from those who are successful. The rest of this chapter is designed to give you the information and wisdom needed to build your own momentum, and encourage the development of the predator mindset. Highlight your favorite quotes and ideas, write them into your personal notebook and use them in each stage of your plan for achievement.

WISDOM FROM A TO Z

Achievement

"Do not be desirous of having things done quickly. Do not look at small advantages. Desire to have things done quickly prevents their being done thoroughly. Looking at small advantages prevents great affairs from being accomplished." – *Confucius*

"The greater the difficulty the more glory in surmounting it. Skillful pilots gain their reputation from storms and tempests." – *Epictetus*

"We live in deeds, not years: In thoughts not breaths; In feelings, not in figures on a dial. We should count time by heart throbs. He most lives Who thinks most, feels the noblest, acts the best." – *David Bailey*

"Success is not measured by what you accomplish, but by the opposition you have encountered, and the courage with which you have maintained the struggle against overwhelming odds." – *Orison Swett Marden*

"Empty pockets never held anyone back. Only empty heads and empty hearts can do that." – *Norman Vincent Peale*

"It's your aptitude, not just your attitude that determines your ultimate altitude." – *Zig Ziglar*

"Every man who is high up loves to think that he has done it all himself; and the wife smiles, and lets it go at that." – *Sir James M. Barrie*

"Having once decided to achieve a certain task, achieve it at all costs of tedium and distaste. The gain in self confidence of having accomplished a tiresome labor is immense." – *Thomas A. Bennett*

"We will either find a way, or make one." – *Hannibal*

"Death comes to all. But great achievements build a monument which shall endure until the sun grows cold." – *George Fabricius*

"Mere longevity is a good thing for those who watch Life from the side lines. For those who play the game, an hour may be a year, a single day's work an achievement for eternity." – *Gabriel Heatter*

"Finish each day and be done with it. You have done what you could. Some blunders and absurdities no doubt crept in; forget them as soon as you can. Tomorrow is a new day; begin it well and serenely and with too high a spirit to be encumbered with your old nonsense."
– *Ralph Waldo Emerson*

"The only way around is through." –*Robert Frost*

"Great things are not done by impulse, but by a series of small things brought together." – *Vincent Van Gogh*

"I feel that the greatest reward for doing is the opportunity to do more."
– Jonas Salk

"If life were measured by accomplishments, most of us would die in infancy."
– A. P. Gouthey

"My mother drew a distinction between achievement and success. She said that achievement is the knowledge that you have studied and worked hard and done the best that is in you. Success is being praised by others. That is nice but not as important or satisfying. Always aim for achievement and forget about success."
– Helen Hayes

"The best job goes to the person who can get it done without passing the buck or coming back with excuses." – *Napoleon Hill*

"A man may fulfill the object of his existence by asking a question he cannot answer, and attempting a task he cannot achieve."
–Oliver Wendell Holmes

"High achievement always takes place in the framework of high expectation."
– Jack Kinder

"Man is always more than he can know of himself; consequently, his accomplishments, time and again, will come as a surprise to him."
– Golo Mann

"Trust yourself. Create the kind of self that you will be happy to live with all your life. Make the most of yourself by fanning the tiny, inner sparks of possibility into flames of achievement." – *Foster C. Mcclellan*

"I am always doing things I can't do, that's how I get to do them."
– *Pablo Picasso*

"The measure of a man is the way he bears up under misfortune."
– *Plutarch*

"The truth of the matter is that there's nothing you can't accomplish if: (1) You clearly decide what it is that you're absolutely committed to achieving, (2) You're willing to take massive action, (3) You notice what's working or not, and (4) You continue to change your approach until you achieve what you want, using whatever life gives you along the way." *–Anthony Robbins*

"Nothing is as difficult as to achieve results in this world if one is filled full of great tolerance and the milk of human kindness. The person who achieves must generally be a one-idea individual, concentrated entirely on that one idea, and ruthless in his aspect toward other men and other ideas."
–Corinne Roosevelt Robinson

"The will to win, the desire to succeed, the urge to reach your full potential... these are the keys that will unlock the door to personal excellence."
– *Eddie Robinson*

"The average estimate themselves by what they do, the above average by what they are." – *Johann Friedrich Von Schiller*

"Disciplining yourself to do what you know is right and important, although difficult, is the high road to pride, self-esteem, and personal satisfaction."
– *Brian Tracy*

"Never mistake activity for achievement." – *John Wooden*

Attitude

"Two men look out the same prison bars; one sees mud and the other stars."
– Frederick Langbridge

"Any fact facing us is not as important as our attitude toward it, for that determines our success or failure. The way you think about a fact may defeat you before you ever do anything about it. You are overcome by the fact because you think you are." **– Norman Vincent Peale**

"To different minds, the same world is a hell, and a heaven."
– Ralph Waldo Emerson

"Always look at what you have left. Never look at what you have lost."
– Robert H. Schuller

"If you believe you can, you probably can. If you believe you won't, you most assuredly won't. Belief is the ignition switch that gets you off the launching pad."
–Denis Waitley

"Ability is what you're capable of doing. Motivation determines what you do. Attitude determines how well you do it."**– Lou Holtz**

"Holding on to anger is like grasping a hot coal with the intent of throwing it at someone else; you are the one who gets burned."**– Buddha**

"The optimist sees opportunity in every danger; the pessimist sees danger in every opportunity." **– Winston Churchill**

"Our attitudes control our lives. Attitudes are a secret power working twenty-four hours a day, for good or bad. It is of paramount importance that we know how to harness and control this great force." **– Tom Blandi**

"Minds are like parachutes - they only function when open."

–Thomas Dewar

"A great attitude does much more than turn on the lights in our worlds; it seems to magically connect us to all sorts of serendipitous opportunities that were somehow absent before the change."*– Earl Nightingale*

"And now here is my secret, a very simple secret; it is only with the heart that one can see rightly, what is essential is invisible to the eye."

– Antoine de Exupery

"The greatest discovery of my generation is that human beings can alter their lives by altering their attitudes of mind." *– William James*

"I am convinced that attitude is the key to success or failure in almost any of life's endeavors. Your attitude–your perspective, your outlook, how you feel about yourself, how you feel about other people–determines your priorities, your actions, your values. Your attitude determines how you interact with other people and how you interact with yourself."*– Carolyn Warner*

"Eagles come in all shapes and sizes, but you will recognize them chiefly by their attitudes." *– Charles Prestwich Scott*

"Attitude is more important than the past, than education, than money, than circumstances, than what people do or say. It is more important than appearance, giftedness, or skill." *– Charles Swindoll*

Character

"Always do right - this will gratify some and astonish the rest."

–Mark Twain

"Of all the properties which belong to honorable men, not one is so highly prized as that of character." *–Henry Clay*

"Die when I may, I want it said by those who knew me best that I always plucked a thistle and planted a flower where I thought a flower would grow."
-Abraham Lincoln

"Judge of your natural character by what you do in your dreams."
-Ralph Waldo Emerson

"There is nothing in which people more betray their character than in what they laugh at." *–Goethe*

"It's really a wonder that I haven't dropped all my ideals, because they seem so absurd and impossible to carry out. Yet I keep them, because in spite of everything I still believe that people are really good at heart."
-Anne Frank

"Character cannot be developed in ease and quiet. Only through experiences of trial and suffering can the soul be strengthened, vision cleared, ambition inspired and success achieved."
-Helen Keller

"Who you are speaks so loudly I can't hear what you're saying."
-Ralph Waldo Emerson

"That which does not kill me, makes me stronger."
–SEAL Team saying

"Kindness in words creates confidence
Kindness in thinking creates profoundness
Kindness in giving creates love."
-Lao-tzu

"Be kind, for everyone you meet is fighting a harder battle."
-Plato

Control

―――

"Warriors take chances. Like everyone else, they fear failing, but they refuse to let fear control them." – *Ancient Samurai saying*

"Flow with whatever is happening and let your mind be free. Stay centered by accepting whatever you are doing. This is the ultimate."
– Chuang Tzu

"No man is fit to command another that cannot command himself."
– William Penn

"No one can make you jealous, angry, vengeful, or greedy - unless you let him." –
Napoleon Hill

"Your brain shall be your servant instead of your master, You will rule it instead of allowing it to rule you." – *Charles E. Popplestone*

"Never allow anyone to rain on your parade and thus cast a pall of gloom and defeat on the entire day. Remember that no talent, no self-denial, no brains, no character, are required to set up in the fault-finding business. Nothing external can have any power over you unless you permit it. Your time is too precious to be sacrificed in wasted days combating the menial forces of hate, jealousy, and envy. Guard your fragile life carefully. Only God can shape a flower, but any foolish child can pull it to pieces."
– Og Mandino

"Nature has placed mankind under the government of two sovereign masters, pain and pleasure... they govern us in all we do, in all we say, in all we think: every effort we can make to throw off our subjection, will serve but to demonstrate and confirm it." – *John Bentham*

"Nothing gives a person so much advantage over another as to remain always cool and unruffled under all circumstances." – *Thomas Jefferson*

"You cannot prevent the birds of sorrow from flying over your head, but you can prevent them from building nests in your hair."
– Chinese Proverb

Determination

"The man who can drive himself further once the effort gets painful is the man who will win." – *Roger Bannister*

"The spirit, the will to win, and the will to excel are the things that endure. These qualities are so much more important than the events that occur."
– Vince Lombardi

"The difference between the impossible and the possible lies in a person's determination." – *Tommy Lasorda*

"Nothing great will ever be achieved without great men, and men are great only if they are determined to be so." – *Charles De Gaulle*

"If your determination is fixed, I do not counsel you to despair. Few things are impossible to diligence and skill. Great works are performed not by strength, but perseverance." – *Samuel Johnson*

"What this power is I cannot say; all I know is that it exists and it becomes available only when a man is in that state of mind in which he knows exactly what he wants and is fully determined not to quit until he finds it."
– Alexander Graham Bell

"I am doing a great work and I cannot come down. Why should the work stop while I leave it and come down to you?" *– Bible*

"Nothing can resist the human will that will stake even its existence on its stated purpose." *– Benjamin Disraeli*

"The longer I live, the more I am certain that the great difference between the great and the insignificant, is energy – invincible determination – a purpose once fixed, and then death or victory."
– Sir Thomas Fowell Buxton

"You can do what you have to do, and sometimes you can do it even better than you think you can." *– Jimmy Carter*

"We will either find a way, or make one!" *– Hannibal*

"A determined soul will do more with a rusty monkey wrench than a loafer will accomplish with all the tools in a machine shop."
– Robert Hughes

"Every worthwhile accomplishment, big or little, has its stages of drudgery and triumph; a beginning, a struggle and a victory." *– Ghandi*

"Bear in mind, if you are going to amount to anything, that your success does not depend upon the brilliancy and the impetuosity with which you take hold, but upon the ever lasting and sanctified bulldoggedness with which you hang on after you have taken hold." *– Dr. A. B. Meldrum*

"A failure establishes only this, that our determination to succeed was not strong enough. "– *John Christian Bovee*

"The price of success is hard work, dedication to the job at hand, and the determination that whether we win or lose, we have applied the best of ourselves to the task at hand." – *Vince Lombardi*

"It takes a little courage, and a little self-control. And some grim determination, If you want to reach the goal. It takes a great deal of striving, and a firm and stern-set chin. No matter what the battle, if you really want to win, there's no easy path to glory, There is no road to fame. Life, however we may view it, Is no simple parlor game; But its prizes call for fighting, For endurance and for grit; For a rugged disposition that will not quit."—*Navy SEAL Masterchief*

Discipline

"In reading the lives of great men, I found that the first victory they won was over themselves...self-discipline with all of them came first."
– *Harry S. Truman*

"If you will discipline yourself to make your mind self-sufficient you will thereby be least vulnerable to injury from the outside."
– *Critias of Athens*

"He conquers twice who conquers himself in victory" – *Jyrus*

"It is better to conquer yourself than to win a thousand battles. Then the victory is yours. It cannot be taken from you, not by angels or by demons, heaven or hell."
– *Buddha*

"What it lies in our power to do, it lies in our power not to do."
– *Aristotle*

"The first and the best victory is to conquer self."– *Plato*

"First we form habits, then they form us. Conquer your bad habits or they will conquer you."– *Rob Gilbert*

"The great end of education is to discipline rather than to furnish the mind; to train it to the use of its own powers, rather than fill it with the accumulation of others." – *Tyron Edwards*

"No man or woman has achieved an effective personality who is not self-disciplined. Such discipline must not be an end in itself, but must be directed to the development of resolute Christian character."
– John S. Bonnell

"If you do not conquer self, you will be conquered by self."
– Napoleon Hill

"No horse gets anywhere until he is harnessed. No stream or gas drives anything until it is confined. No Niagara is ever turned into light and power until it is tunneled. No life ever grows great until it is focused, dedicated, disciplined."
– Harry Emerson Fosdick

"The only discipline that lasts is self discipline." – *Bum Phillips*

"A colt is worth little if it does not break its halter." – *Proverb*

"Nothing of importance is ever achieved without discipline. I feel myself sometimes not wholly in sympathy with some modern educational theorists, because I think that they underestimate the part that discipline plays. But the discipline you have in your life should be one determined by your own desires and your own needs, not put upon you by society or authority."
– Bertrand Russell

"He who lives without discipline dies without honor."
– Icelandic Proverb

Focus

"The human mind is not rich enough to drive manyhorses abreast and wants one general scheme, under which it strives to bring everything."
– George Santayana

"The shortest way to do many things is to do only one thing at a time."
– Mozart

"Nothing focuses the mind better than the constant sight of a competitor who wants to wipe you off the map." *– Wayne Calloway*

"Most people have no idea of the giant capacity we can immediately command when we focus all of our resources on mastering a single area of our lives."
– Anthony Robbins

"The successful warrior is the average man, with laser-like focus."
– Bruce Lee

"If you focus on results, you will never change. If you focus on change, you will get results." *– Jack Dixon*

"Concentration is the ability to think about absolutely nothing when it is absolutely necessary." *– Ray Knight*

"Get out of the blocks, run your race, stay relaxed. If you run your race, you'll win. Channel your energy. Focus." *– Carol Lewis*

"Determine what specific goal you want to achieve. Then dedicate yourself to its attainment with unswerving singleness of purpose, the trenchant zeal of a crusader." *– Paul J. Meyer*

"Often he who does too much does too little." *– Italian Proverb*

"To succeed at the level I want to… you have to be focused and serious." *– Kent Steffes*

"He who dares….Wins!" *– British SAS motto*

Goals

"Without goals, and plans to reach them, you are like a ship that has set sail with no destination." *– Fitzhugh Dodson*

"Aim for the top. There is plenty of room there. There are so few at the top it is almost lonely there." *– Samuel Insull*

"The goal you set must be challenging. At the same time, it should be realistic and attainable, not impossible to reach. It should be challenging enough to make you stretch, but not so far that you break." *– Rick Hansen*

"You must have long term goals to keep you from being frustrated by short term failures." *– Charles C. Noble*

"What you get by achieving your goals is not as important as what you become by achieving your goals." *– Zig Ziglar*

"First say to yourself what you would be; and then do what you have to do." *– Epictetus*

"The person with a fixed goal, a clear picture of his desire, or an ideal always before him, causes it, through repetition, to be buried deeply in his subconscious mind and is thus enabled, thanks to its generative and sustaining power, to realize his goal in a minimum of time and with a minimum of physical effort. Just pursue the thought unceasingly. Step by step you will achieve realization, for all your faculties and powers become directed to that end." – *Claude M. Bristol*

"If you don't know where you are going, you might wind up someplace else."
– *Yogi Berra*

"Go for the moon. If you don't get it, you'll still be heading for a star."
– *Willis Reed*

"It is those who concentrate on but one thing at a time who advance in this world." – *Og Mandino*

"Our goals can only be reached through a vehicle of a plan, in which we must fervently believe, and upon which we must vigorously act. There is no other route to success." – *Stephen A. Brennan*

"If I've got correct goals, and if I keep pursuing them the best way I know how, everything else falls into line. If I do the right thing right, I'm going to succeed."
– *Dan Dierdorf*

"If you raise your children to feel that they can accomplish any goal or task they decide upon, you will have succeeded as a parent and you will have given your children the greatest of all blessings."– *Brian Tracy*

"We aim above the mark to hit the mark." – *Ralph Waldo Emerson*

"It is for us to pray not for tasks equal to our powers, but for powers equal to our tasks, to go forward with a great desire forever beating at the door of our hearts as we travel toward our distant goal."– *Helen Keller*

"Difficulties increase the nearer we approach the goal."
– Johann Wolfgang Von Goethe

"Decide what you want, decide what you are willing to exchange for it. Establish your priorities and go to work." *– H. L. Hunt*

"From a certain point onward there is no longer any turning back. That is the point that must be reached." *– Franz Kafka*

"Nothing can add more power to your life than concentrating all your energies on a limited set of targets." *– Nido Qubein*

"Setting goals for your game is an art. The trick is in setting them at the right level neither too low nor too high." *– Greg Norman*

"Nothing can stop the man with the right mental attitude from achieving his goal; nothing on earth can help the man with the wrong mental attitude."
– Thomas Jefferson

"My philosophy of life is that if we make up our mind what we are going to make of our lives, then work hard toward that goal, we never lose – somehow we win out." *– Ronald Reagan*

"Having an exciting destination is like setting a needle in your compass. From then on, the compass knows only one point-its ideal. And it will faithfully guide you there through the darkest nights and fiercest storms." *– Daniel Boone*

Greatness

"There are no great men, only great challenges that ordinary men are forced by circumstances to meet." *– William F. Halsey*

"Greatness does not approach him who is forever looking down."

– Hitopadesa

"No great man ever complains of want of opportunity."

– Ralph Waldo Emerson

"Great men are true men, the men in whom nature has succeeded. They are not extraordinary – they are in the true order. It is the other species of men who are not what they ought to be." *– Henri Frederic Amiel*

"Be not afraid of greatness; some are born great, some achieve greatness, and others have greatness thrust upon them." *– William Shakespeare*

"No great man lives in vain. The history of the world is but the biography of great men." *– Thomas Carlyle*

"Man is only truly great when he acts from his passions."

– Benjamin Disraeli

"In our society those who are in reality superior in intelligence can be accepted by their fellows only if they pretend they are not."

– Marya Mannes

"Great men are like eagles, and build their nest on some lofty solitude."

–   Arthur Schopenhauer

"Well, I wouldn't say that I was in the great class, but I had a great time while I was trying to be great." *– Harry S. Truman*

Habit

"We are what we repeatedly do. Excellence then, is not an act, but a habit."

– Aristotle

"A nail is driven out by another nail. Habit is overcome by habit."
– Desiderius Erasmus

"First we form habits, then they form us. Conquer your bad habits or they will conquer you."*– Rob Gilbert*

"Tell me what you eat, and I will tell you what you are."
– Anthelme Brillat-Savarin

"Power is the faculty or capacity to act, the strength and potency to accomplish something. It is the vital energy to make choices and decisions. It also includes the capacity to overcome deeply embedded habits and to cultivate higher, more effective ones."*– Stephen R. Covey*

"Winning is a habit. Unfortunately, so is losing."
– Vince Lombardi

"Your net worth to the world is usually determined by what remains after your bad habits are subtracted from your good ones."
– Benjamin Franklin

"Habits...the only reason they persist is that they are offering some satisfaction...You allow them to persist by not seeking any other, better form of satisfying the same needs. Every habit, good or bad, is acquired and learned in the same way - by finding that it is a means of satisfaction."*– Juliene Berk*

"Once you learn to quit, it becomes a habit." *– Vince Lombardi*

"I never could have done what I have done without the habits of punctuality, order, and diligence, without the determination to concentrate myself on one subject at a time."*– Charles Dickens*

"It is hard to let old beliefs go. They are familiar. We are comfortable with them and have spent years building systems and developing habits that depend on them. Like a man who has worn eyeglasses so long that he forgets he has them on, we forget that the world looks to us the way it does because we have become used to seeing it that way through a particular set of lenses. Today, however, we need new lenses. And we need to throw the old ones away."– *Kenich Ohmae*

"Good habits result from resisting temptation." – *Indian Proverb*

"As a twig is bent the tree inclines." – *Virgil*

"Thoughts lead on to purposes; purposes go forth in action; actions form habits; habits decide character; and character fixes our destiny."
– *Tryon Edwards*

Health

"Ill-health, of body or of mind, is defeat. Health alone is victory. Let all men, if they can manage it, contrive to be healthy!" – *Thomas Carlyle*

"He who enjoys good health is rich, though he knows it not."
– *Italian Proverb*

"To get rich never risk your health. For it is the truth that health is the wealth of wealth." – *Richard Baker*

"The ingredients of health and long life, are great temperance, open air, easy labor, and little care." – *Sir Philip Sidney*

"To insure good health: Eat lightly, breathe deeply, live moderately, cultivate cheerfulness, and maintain an interest in life."
– *William Londen*

"A man's health can be judged by which he takes two at a time – pills or stairs."
– *Joan Welsh*

"The sovereign invigorator of the body is exercise, and of all the exercises walking is the best." – *Thomas Jefferson*

"The human body has been designed to resist an infinite number of changes and attacks brought about by its environment. The secret of good health lies in successful adjustment to changing stresses on the body."
– *Harry J. Johnson*

Knowledge

"I am enough of an artist to draw freely upon my imagination. Imagination is more important than knowledge. Knowledge is limited. Imagination encircles the world."– *Albert Einstein*

"Every mind was made for growth, for knowledge, and its nature is sinned against when it is doomed to ignorance."
– *William Ellery Channing*

"You can swim all day in the Sea of Knowledge and still come out completely dry. Most people do."– *Norman Juster*

"Knowledge is power and enthusiasm pulls the switch."
– *Steve Droke*

"Not to know is bad, not to wish to know is worse."
– *Nigerian Proverb*

"The old believe everything; the middle aged suspect everything: the young know everything."– *Oscar Wilde*

"Where is the Life we have lost in living?

Where is the wisdom we have lost in knowledge?

Where is the knowledge we have lost in information?"

– T. S. Eliot

"Zeal without knowledge is fire without light."*– Thomas Fuller*

"The essence of knowledge is, having it, to apply it; not having it, to confess your ignorance." *– Confucius*

"Today knowledge has power. It controls access to opportunity and advancement." *– Peter F. Drucker*

"God grant that not only the love of liberty but a thorough knowledge of the rights of man may pervade all the nations of the earth, so that a philosopher may set his foot anywhere on its surface and say: This is my country!" *– Benjamin Franklin*

"Knowledge is of two kinds: We know a subject ourselves, or we know where we can find information about it."

– Samuel Johnson

"The hunger and thirst for knowledge, the keen delight in the chase, the good humored willingness to admit that the scent was false, the eager desire to get on with the work, the cheerful resolution to go back and begin again, the broad good sense, the unaffected modesty, the imperturbable temper, the gratitude for any little help that was given – all these will remain in my memory though I cannot paint them for others".

– Frederic William Maitland

"It is nothing for one to know something unless another knows you know it."

– Persian Proverb

"To know that we know what we know, and that we do not know what we do not know, that is true knowledge."

– Henry David Thoreau

"The trouble with the world is not that people know too little, but that they know so many things that ain't so." *– Mark Twain*

"We live on an island surrounded by a sea of ignorance. As our island of knowledge grows, so does the shore of our ignorance."

– John Archibald Wheeler

Leadership

"The boss drives people; the leader coaches them. The boss depends on authority; the leader on good will. The boss inspires fear; the leader inspires enthusiasm. The boss says "I"; The leader says "WE". The boss fixes the blame for the breakdown; the leader fixes the breakdown. The boss says, "GO"; the leader says "LET'S GO!" *– H. Gordon Selfridge*

"Leaders aren't born, they are made. And they are made just like anything else, through hard work. And that's the price we'll have to pay to achieve that goal, or any goal." *– Vince Lombardi*

"I am personally convinced that one person can be a change catalyst, a "transformer" in any situation, any organization. Such an individual is yeast that can leaven an entire loaf. It requires vision, initiative, patience, respect, persistence, courage, and faith to be a transforming leader."

– Stephen R. Covey

"A boss creates fear, a leader confidence.

A boss fixes blame, a leader corrects mistakes.

A boss knows all, a leader asks questions.

A boss makes work drudgery, a leader makes it interesting.

A boss is interested in himself or herself, a leader is interested in the group."

– Russell H. Ewing

"One of the true tests of leadership is the ability to recognize a problem before it becomes an emergency." **– Arnold Glasow**

"People ask the difference between a leader and a boss. The leader works in the open, and the boss in covert. The leader leads, and the boss drives."

– Theodore Roosevelt

"A leader is best

When people barely know he exists,

When his work is done, his aim fulfilled,

They will say:

We did it ourselves."**– Lao-Tzu**

"A leader takes people where they want to go. A great leader takes people where they don't necessarily want to go, but ought to be."**—Rosalynn Carter**

"Do not follow where the path may lead. Go instead where there is no path and leave a trail."**– Muriel Strode**

"The challenge of leadership is to be strong, but not rude; be kind, but not weak; be bold, but not bully; be thoughtful, but not lazy; be humble, but not timid; be proud, but not arrogant; have humor, but without folly". **– Jim Rohn**

"The best executive is the one who has sense enough to pick good men to do what he wants done, and self-restraint enough to keep from meddling with them while they do it."**– Theodore Roosevelt**

"A man who wants to lead the orchestra must turn his back on the crowd."

– James Crook

"Leadership is getting someone to do what they don't want to do, to achieve what they want to achieve."*– Tom Landry*

"Leadership is the art of getting someone else to do something you want done because he wants to do it."*– Dwight D. Eisenhower*

"Outstanding leaders go out of their way to boost the self-esteem of their personnel. If people believe in themselves, it's amazing what they can accomplish." *– Sam Walton*

A true leader has the confidence to stand alone, the courage to make tough decisions, and the compassion to listen to the needs of others. He does not set out to be a leader, but becomes one by the quality of his actions and the integrity of his intent." *– Douglas McCarther*

"You manage things; you lead people."

– Rear Admiral Grace Murray Hopper

"If I advance, follow me! If I retreat, kill me! If I die, avenge me!"

– Francois De La Rochefoucauld

"I have three precious things which I hold fast and prize. The first is gentleness; the second is frugality; the third is humility, which keeps me from putting myself before others. Be gentle and you can be bold; be frugal and you can be liberal; avoid putting yourself before others and you can become a leader among men." –

Lao-Tzu

"It is very comforting to believe that leaders who do terrible things are, in fact, mad. That way, all we have to do is make sure we don't put psychotics in high places and we've got the problem solved"

– Thomas Wolfe

"An army of deer would be more formidable commanded by a lion, than a an army of lions commanded by a stag." **– Viking Proverb**

Performance

"Performance, and performance alone, dictates the predator in any food chain."

– SEAL Team saying

"Too aim is not enough, you must hit!" **– German Proverb**

"Slumps are like a soft bed. They're easy to get into and hard to get out of."

– Johnny Bench

"If a man or woman is born ten years sooner or later, their whole aspect and performance shall be different." **– Johann Wolfgang Von Goethe**

"I like to be against the odds. I'm not afraid to be lonely at the top. With me, it's just the satisfaction of the game. Just performance."

– Barry Bonds

"Great works are done when one is not calculating and thinking."

– Daisetz T. Suzuki

"There's no such thing as coulda, shoulda, or woulda. If you shoulda and coulda, you woulda done it." **– Pat Riley**

You have to perform at a consistently higher level than others. That's the mark of a true professional." **– Joe Paterno**

Perseverance

—————————————————————————

"On the mountains of truth you can never climb in vain: either you will reach a point higher up today, or you will be training your powers so that you will be able to climb higher tomorrow." – *Friedrich Nietzsche*

"In the confrontation between the stream and the rock, the stream always wins– not through strength but by perseverance." – *H. Jackson Brown*

"People of mediocre ability sometimes achieve outstanding success because they don't know when to quit. Most men succeed because they are determined to."
– George E. Allen

"Perseverance is more prevailing than violence; and many things which cannot be overcome when they are together, yield themselves up when taken little by little."
– Plutarch

"Perseverance is not a long race; it is many short races one after another."
– Walter Elliott

"It's not so important who starts the game but who finishes it."
– John Wooden

"Most of the important things in the world have been accomplished by people who have kept on trying when there seemed to be no help at all."*– Dale Carnegie*

"All great masters are chiefly distinguished by the power of adding a second, a third, and perhaps a fourth step in a continuous line. Many a man has taken the first step. With every additional step you enhance immensely the value of your first." – *Ralph Waldo Emerson*

"Consider the postage stamp: its usefulness consists in the ability to stick to one thing until it gets there."*– Josh Billings*

"Some men give up their designs when they have almost reached the goal; While others, on the contrary, obtain a victory by exerting, at the last moment, more vigorous efforts than ever before."– *Herodotus*

"Nothing in the world can take the place of persistence. Talent will not; nothing is more common than unsuccessful men with talent. Genius will not; unrewarded genius is almost a proverb. Education will not; the world is full of educated derelicts. Persistence and determination alone are omnipotent. The slogan, 'press on' has solved, and always will solve, the problems of the human race."

– Calvin Coolidge

"I do not think there is any other quality so essential to success of any kind as the quality of perseverance. It overcomes almost everything, even nature."

– John D. Rockefeller

"Success is not final, failure is not fatal: it is the courage to continue that counts."– *Winston Churchill*

"Success seems to be connected with action. Successful men keep moving. They make mistakes, but they don't quit."– *Conrad Hilton*

"If I had to select one quality, one personal characteristic that I regard as being most highly correlated with success, whatever the field, I would pick the trait of persistence. Determination. The will to endure to the end, to get knocked down seventy times and get up off the floor saying, "Here comes number seventy-one!"

– Richard M. Devos

"Good ideas are not adopted automatically. They must be driven into practice with courageous patience."– *Admiral Hyman Rickover*

"For a righteous man falls seven times, and rises again."
[Proverbs 24:16] – *Bible*

"He who asks of life nothing but the improvement of his own nature… is less liable than anyone else to miss and waste life."
– Henri Frederic Amiel

Strength

"Fire is the test of gold; adversity, of strong men.*– Seneca*

Strength does not come from physical capacity. It comes from an indomitable will."*– Mahatma Gandhi*

"I love the man that can smile in trouble, that can gather strength from distress, and grow brave by reflection. 'Tis the business of little minds to shrink, but he whose heart is firm, and whose conscience approves his conduct, will pursue his principles unto death."*– Thomas Paine*

"We acquire the strength we have overcome."
– Ralph Waldo Emerson

"Don't hit at all if it is honorably possible to avoid hitting, but never hit soft."
– Theodore Roosevelt

"Strength is a matter of a made up mind." *– John Beecher*

"Don't expect to build up the weak by pulling down the strong."
– Calvin Coolidge

"Nothing is so strong as gentleness, and nothing is so gentle as true strength."
– Ralph Sockman

"What the lion cannot manage to do the fox can."
– German Proverb

"Do not pray for easy lives. Pray to be stronger men! Do not pray for tasks equal to your powers. Pray for power equal to your tasks."– *Phillips Brooks*

"Few men during their lifetime come anywhere near exhausting the resources dwelling within them. There are deep wells of strength that are never used"
– Richard E. Byrd

"Greatness lies not in being strong, but in the right use of strength."
– Henry Ward Beecher

"The burden is equal to the horse's strength." *– The Talmud*

"It is truly said: It does not take much strength to do things, but it requires great strength to decide what to do. *– Chow Ching*

"Only actions give life strength; only moderation gives it charm."
– Jean Paul Richter

"Our real problem, then, is not our strength today; it is rather the vital necessity of action today to ensure our strength tomorrow."
– Dwight D. Eisenhower

"Life only demands from you the strength you possess. Only one feat is possible–
not to have run away."– *Dag Hammarskjold*

"Strong men can always afford to be gentle. Only the weak are intent on giving as good as they get."– *Elbert Hubbard*

Survival

"Survival, with honor, that outmoded and all-important word, is as difficult as ever and as all-important to a writer. Those who do not last are always more beloved since no one has to see them in their long, dull, unrelenting, no-quarter-given-and-no-quarter-received, fights that they make to do something as they believe it should be done before they die. Those who die or quit early and easy and with every good reason are preferred because they are understandable and human. Failure and well-disguised cowardice are more human and more beloved." *– Ernest Hemingway*

"The more we exploit nature, The more our options are reduced, until we have only one: to fight for survival." *– Morris K. Udall*

"Nobody is stronger, nobody is weaker than someone who came back. There is nothing you can do to such a person because whatever you could do is less than what has already been done to him. We have already paid the price."
– Elie Wiesel

"Once one determines that he or she has a mission in life, that's it's not going to be accomplished without a great deal of pain, and that the rewards in the end may not outweigh the pain –if you recognize historically that always happens, then when it comes, you survive it." *– Richard M. Nixon*

"The consciousness of being deemed dead, is next to the presumable unpleasantness of being so in reality. One feels like his own ghost unlawfully tenanting a defunct carcass." *– Herman Melville*

Teamwork

"When two people meet, there are really six people present. There is each man as he sees himself, each man as he wants to be seen, and each man as he really is."
– Michael De Saintamo

"Alone we can do so little; together we can do so much." *– Helen Keller*

"Teamwork is the ability to work together toward a common vision. The ability to direct individual accomplishments toward organizational objectives. It is the fuel that allows common people to attain uncommon results."– *Andrew Carnegie*

"Coming together is a beginning, staying together is progress, and working together is success." – *Henry Ford*

"The achievements of an organization are the results of the combined effort of each individual." – *Vince Lombardi*

"The nice thing about teamwork is that you always have others on your side."
– *Margaret Carty*

"When your team is winning, be ready to be tough, because winning can make you soft. On the other hand, when your team is losing, stick by them. Keep believing." – *Bo Schembechler*

"Individuals play the game, but teams beat the odds."
– *SEAL Team saying*

"The way a team plays as a whole determines its success. You may have the greatest bunch of individual stars in the world, but if they don't play together, the club won't be worth a dime." – *Babe Ruth*

"If a team is to reach its potential, each player must be willing to subordinate his personal goals to the good of the team."
–*Bud Wilkinson*

"People have been known to achieve more as a result of working with others than against them." – *Dr. Allan Fromme*

"When he took time to help the man up the mountain, lo, he scaled it himself."
– *Tibetan Proverb*

Victory

"The softest things in the world overcome the hardest things in the world."
– Lao-Tzu

"The ultimate victory in competition is derived from the inner satisfaction of knowing that you have done your best and that you have gotten the most out of what you had to give." *– Howard Cosell*

"The will to conquer is the first condition of victory." *– Ferdinand Foch*

"Men talk as if victory were something fortunate. Work is victory."
–Ralph Waldo Emerson

"I would rather lose in a cause that will some day win, than win in a cause that will some day lose!" *– Woodrow T. Wilson*

"The most dangerous moment comes with victory."
– Napoleon Bonaparte

"The people who remained victorious were less like conquerors than conquered."
– St. Augustine

"One may know how to gain a victory, and know not how to use it."
– Pedro Calderón de la Barca

Willpower

"Strength does not come from physical capacity. It comes from an indomitable will." *– Mahatma Gandhi*

"Will power is to the mind like a strong blind man who carries on his shoulders a lame man who can see." *– Arthur Schopenhauer*

"The world is full of willing people, some willing to work, the rest willing to let them." – ***Robert Frost***

"Great souls have wills; feeble ones have only wishes."
– ***Chinese Proverb***

"A man can do all things if he but wills them."
– ***Leon Battista Alberti***

"People do not lack strength; they lack will." – ***Victor Hugo***

"What you have to do and the way you have to do it is incredibly simple. Whether you are willing to do it, that's another matter."
– ***Peter F. Drucker***

"Will is character in action." – ***William Mcdougall***

"It is fatal to enter any war without the will to win it."
– ***Douglas Macarthur***

"Free will and determinism are like a game of cards. The hand that is dealt you is determinism. The way you play your hand is free will." – ***Norman Cousins***

"Self-will so ardent and active that it will break a world to pieces to make a stool to sit on." – ***Richard Cecil***

"They ean conquer who believe they can. He has not learned the first lesson in life who does not every day surmount a fear."
– ***Ralph Waldo Emerson***

Winning

"I count him braver who overcomes his desires than him who conquers his enemies; for the hardest victory is over self."

– Aristotle

"Winning is everything, to win is all there is. Only those poor souls buried beneath the battlefield understand this."

– SEAL Team saying

"All right Mister, let me tell you what winning means... you're willing to go longer, work harder, give more than anyone else."

– Vince Lombardi

"Winning is not everything, but the effort to win is." *– Zig Ziglar*

"The reason most people never reach their goals is that they don't define them, learn about them, or even seriously consider them as believable or achievable. Winners can tell you where they are going, what they plan to do along the way, and who will be sharing the adventure with them."

– Denis Waitley

"History has demonstrated that the most notable winners usually encountered heartbreaking obstacles before they triumphed. They won because they refused to become discouraged by their defeats."

– Bertie C. Forbes

"The man who can drive himself further once the effort gets painful is the man who will win."*– Roger Bannister*

"You can't be a winner and be afraid to lose."*– Charles Lynch*

"Those that know how to win are much more numerous than those who know how to make proper use of their victories." – ***Polybius***

"The harder the conflict, the more glorious the triumph."
– Thomas Paine

"Guts are a combination of confidence, courage, conviction, strength of character, stick-to-itiveness, pugnaciousness, backbone, and intestinal fortitude. They are mandatory for anyone who wants to get to and stay at the top." – ***D. A. Benton***

"Only a man who knows what it is like to be defeated can reach down to the bottom of his soul and come up with the extra ounce of power it takes to win when the match is even."
– Muhammad Ali

"The first man gets the oyster, the second man gets the shell."
– Andrew Carnegie

"I am not bound to win, but I am bound to be true. I am not bound to succeed, but I am bound to live by the light that I have. I must stand with anybody that stands right, and stand with him while he is right, and part with him when he goes wrong." *– Abraham Lincoln*

"Never let defeat have the last word." —*Tibetan Proverb*

"There is no victory at bargain basement prices."
– Dwight David Eisenhower

"There are many victories worse than a defeat."*– George Eliot*

CHAPTER 7 -100 SECRETS OF POWER LIVING

"Self-respect is the fruit of discipline; the sense of dignity grows with the ability to say NO to oneself."

-Abraham J. Heshel

There are thousands of little secrets and techniques that can be used to change the way we live, but I am not going to insult your intelligence by bombarding you with new age rhetoric or psychological terms. The 100 secrets of power living are facts and concepts that are used and practiced everyday by some of the most elite commando units on this planet. I have taken these powerful techniques and concepts and altered them for everyday use. Keep an open mind, take notes, think deeply, and try implementing a few each day.

The world's most successful people use these concepts and techniques every single day to advance to the top of the human food chain. Start creating an aura of positive energy that radiates and touches everyone around you. Use these secrets of power living as a tool for controlling the changes in your life.

1. One hour a day

Set aside one hour each morning for personal development work. Visualize your day, listen to motivational music and tapes, or read inspirational books or statements to gain positive focus and clarity of purpose.

2. Keep a journal or notebook

We all have thoughts, ideas, tasks, and inspirations that pop into our heads throughout the day. Keep a small journal with you at all times to record these bursts of mental energy.

3. Exercise

Do something each and every day to enhance your physical health. What you do is not as important as how much you do. Make a steady commitment to include some form of physical activity into your daily schedule. Include a friend, spouse, or partner into your exercise routine to provide support and motivation. Do 50 sit-ups and 50 push-ups every morning before you hit the shower; this will not only wake you up, but also generate a flow of positive energy throughout your body and mind.

4. Sleep less

Most people do not need more than seven hours of sleep to maintain peak health. Try getting up one hour earlier for seven days and it will develop into a powerful routine. Imagine having an extra seven hours a week to spend on the things you want. This is one of the most powerful and life changing commitments you can make to become more productive and organized.

5. Learn to sit still and listen

Most people don't even spend two minutes a week in total silence and peace. Enjoy the power of silence and tranquility for at least

10 minutes a day. Reflect on where your life is going and what you are doing to master control of it. Practice the skill of sitting quietly in a peaceful and powerful place.

6. Laughter as medicine

Learn to laugh for at least five minutes a day. Laughter activates potent chemicals in our bodies that elevate us to a happy, balanced, and carefree state. Some therapies actually use laughter to heal a person's illness and it is a wonderful drug for life's dose of reality. Purchase a funny tape or book to keep you laughing throughout the day. Laughter as medicine will create an environment of health and vitality.

7. Master time management

There are approximately 672 hours in one month. I am sure you can allot 10 of these toward the achievement of the goals you desire. Become ruthless with your time. Treasure and guard each minute as if it were your last. Plan around your top priorities and focus on doing immediate, short term, and long term goals that you wish to accomplish. Buy an electronic or paper organizer; tack up planning boards, calendars, and to-do lists in your house and at work. Never forget what matters most to you and give that the majority of your time.

8. Positive surroundings

Associate with only positive, friendly, and focused people who do not drain your time and energy. Become acquainted with people of great success and knowledge. Have books in your library about self-improvement, positive attitudes, wealth, health, religion, and success.

9. Picture your reward

Have pictures of all the things you want to have or become. Cut out pictures of houses, properties, vehicles, vacations, or of the body you want to have, and carry them with you everyday. Become accustomed to seeing the desired efforts of your labor and you will eventually make them a reality.

10. Learn a new word each day

Have a dictionary on your desk or beside your bed and circle one new word a day. Say this word and its definition five times to yourself and use it in a sentence during the day. This simple technique will not only improve your communication skills, but become an example to everyone around you of your personal commitment and work ethic.

11. Study ancient wisdoms

The secrets to wealth, health, beauty, longevity, and vitality have been in existence for thousands of years. Rap music, fast food, fashion, television, and computers are not secrets to better living. Open your mind to ancient herbs, diets, exercises, breathing techniques, philosophies, and your life will make a dramatic change for the better.

12. Turn off the TV

What medium do you think is responsible for the food we eat, clothes we wear, way we talk, items we purchase, music we listen to, and the hours we spend sitting around? Yep, you guessed it! Television is the most powerful form of mind control known to man. Just as visualization is a powerful technique for our minds, television uses images, tastes, sounds, and fantasy to control what we do and think. Do you and your children a favor by drastically reducing the amount of brain-washing you are exposed to. The average American family watches four hours of television per day. You say that there are not enough minutes in the day to get everything done? Well, here is a way to free-up 240 minutes a day for personal development and quality time with the ones you love. **Unplug the brain-washing machine!**

13. Learn a language

In the SEAL Teams we must be proficient in foreign languages. Nothing stimulates the mind like learning everything possible about a different culture, including the language. Take a course, buy books or tapes, practice with a friend, or visit a country and culture of your interest. It is a wonderful and magnificent world we live in, so take advantage of it and expand your talents and knowledge.

14. Supplement your life

Increase your knowledge of herbs, vitamins, and nutritional supplements. Dramatically reduce your health care costs and sick days, while improving your health, vitality, and longevity. If you like radiation, chemicals, toxins, surgery, and hospitals, just go ahead and ignore this one! Try a cup of Chinese Green Tea with your meals and experience the benefits of this 5,000 year old wonder-drink. There are many excellent books and tapes available that can help explain the tremendous powers of herbs, vitamins, and supplements.

15. Polish your appearance

Start by practicing the principals of physical discipline and spend 30 minutes more each day making sure you present the image of competence, intelligence, and professionalism. Learn how to iron your shirts and pants, get a clean, short haircut, polish your shoes, and prepare ahead for the next workday. Remember that first impressions are the lasting ones.

16. Speak with discipline

It doesn't matter how professional or competent you look, if you swear like a sailor or always have a smart remark, you are advertising your ignorance to everyone. Stop and think about what you want to say before you say it. If you condition yourself to pause before saying anything, people will naturally respond with interest. Take the time to practice and think about what sort of words and body language you wish to use.

17. Breath of life

Good breathing practices will unleash the energy that lies deep inside you. Deep breathing maintains a peak state of both body and mind fitness and health. Ancient breathing practices fully oxygenate the body and recharge you with energy to tackle your demanding tasks. Ancient societies have always used deep breathing techniques to create optimal health, happiness, and mental clarity. Take some time each day to study and practice deep breathing techniques.

18. Positive mental attitude

Having a positive mental attitude about everything in life will allow you to succeed where others have failed. To become an expert in any human activity takes practice and a positive mental attitude. It doesn't matter how bad things are, the person with a never-say-die attitude and positive outlook will always find a way to the top. Practice mental techniques for finding the good in every situation and circumstance. Stop complaining and start looking at what is good and right, instead of bad and wrong. Have an attitude of defiance and perseverance towards failure in all aspects of your life. Focus on erasing or reprogramming negative thoughts and actions.

19. Rebuild character flaws

Every human being has flaws in his character and personality. Use mental discipline to recognize and reprogram those glitches and flaws. Listen to what your spouse, friends, and family say about your behavior and personality. Take a written inventory of your character every 30 days to focus on areas that need improvement. Become aware of your habits, traits, and overall personality.

20. Buy a pet

Have a pet as a best friend. Animals have been shown to greatly reduce stress and improve happiness in humans. Having a pet is one of the best ways to practice responsibility and commitment. Teaching your children to be responsible for taking care of the family pet is an invaluable teaching tool. Learn to appreciate the other inhabitants of our planet and enhance the quality of your life.

21. Goal warfare

Discover what it is you really want out of this life, and go into battle for it. Take time each day to schedule and refocus your efforts in this direction. Start off with small and easy goals, then gear up for the larger battles. Prioritize your energy and efforts toward accomplishing your life's dreams, but always take time to enjoy the little things in life.

22. Strong relationship = strong life

Set aside at least one night each week to be alone with your spouse. Get a babysitter, turn off the television, and focus all of your attention on your life partner. Start really communicating and enjoying the company of this special gift in your life. Behind every successful person lies a strong and supportive spouse.

23. Become the aggressor

We have all heard the saying that "the meek shall inherit the Earth," but have you heard the saying that "it's a dog eat dog world?" Make no mistake about it, we live in a super-competitive world today and only the aggressive and committed come out on top. Look people straight in the eyes when you talk to them, but talk with authority and intelligence. Attack each new day and project with the same ferociousness that a lion uses on its prey. Become a predator of success by going the extra mile, or doing more than is asked of you. Being humble is a virtue, but dominating your enemies and devouring your problems is a way of life.

24. Stop overeating

Eat only what you need and push the rest away. Our society is the most blessed and rich nation on this planet, and it shows! Add money to your bank account and more years to your life by stopping before you are full. The human stomach was not designed to hold and digest more than a handful of food, so think light and small when eating. I eat, I eat some more, I get fat, and therefore I am, should be our national motto. Controlling what and how much we eat is an excellent test for our self-discipline. Welcome the challenge and start power living, instead of power eating.

25. Become the Chameleon

Start imitating the successes of great people and leaders. Study your top-ten most interesting and successful people, and learn what and how they did it. Have a personal role model that inspires you to greatness. Imitate the best virtues and strengths of our world's most respected and successful humans by researching every step they made.

26. Control your emotions

Learn to be emotionally neutral during troublesome times. Control your anger and depression by pausing, then slowly counting to ten. Control and understand the effects of food upon your emotions and personality. Discipline your mind to block out urges and suppress emotions during each conversation. Be emotional when you are with the people you love and trust, but never show weakness to others. See #23 above.

27. Relax and recharge

Nothing drains your energy more than stress and worrying. Create a sanctuary in your house or office that is peaceful, serene, silent, and full of positive energy. Go outside and sit under a tree, or go for a walk in the woods to gather your thoughts, slow your heart rate, and gain clarity of mind. Create a garden that is pleasant in sight, sound, and smell. Schedule 30 minutes each day for relaxation and meditation development. This is one of the most powerful concepts of power living.

28. Pinch pennies

The best way to have money is to save money! You don't have to be frugal to save money, just organized. Take time to really study and investigate your personal finances. Stay at home more often to benefit your relationship and family life. Clip coupons, shop around, take care of what you have and it will take care of you. Start a savings plan that automatically deducts money from your pay. When you begin mastering financial self-discipline, wonderful things happen.

29. *Practice mind control*

Use the techniques of mental reprogramming and thought control to bring a positive energy to your thoughts and actions. Wear a rubber band around your wrist and snap it every time a negative or bad thought comes into your mind; this will program a physical and mental reaction to negativity. Surround yourself with positive images and statements and monitor the information that is allowed to bombard your brain.

30. *Challenge yourself daily*

Set lofty goals and strive to attain them every day. Expect more of yourself than anybody else does. Challenge stimulates the mind and body into positive action. Stop staying "I can't" and start saying "I will". Try to better your last physical or work-related performance and enjoy the benefits of power living.

31. *Master personal management*

Become organized and efficient in all aspects of your life. Schedule time to organize all of your possessions and valuables. Buy a computer or pocket organizer to record and efficiently manage all of your personal and professional matters. Spend 20 minutes each night preparing your clothing, food, and to-do list for the following day.

32. *Relearn your manners*

Practice the codes of personal conduct that your parents or grandparents instilled in you. Say "yes ma'am," or "yes sir" when addressing an older person. Treat people with respect and dignity in every situation. Become someone that your children and family can look up to and respect.

33. Advertise integrity

Behave and talk in the same manner when you are away from your spouse, as you would when you are with your spouse. Self-discipline is about making and keeping personal commitments. Treat your relationship or marriage as the ultimate commitment and example of mutual respect. A man or woman of integrity puts principal and moral ethics in front of pleasure and personal gain. Practice the concept of keeping your promises and doing what is right, instead of what is popular.

34. Be a giver and not a taker

Tithe at church, or give to charities and worthwhile organizations. Do good things for others and others will do good things for you. Become the person that friends can come to in a time of need and watch your personal satisfaction rise.

35. Become a seeker of knowledge

Use the principals of knowledge control to fill your mind and life with useful and interesting information. Take a course at a local college or trade school, learn a new skill each month. Surround yourself with good books and self-improvement literature. You are what you eat, but you act upon what you know.

36. Take time to reflect

Schedule 10 minutes each day to pause and reflect upon your performance in all aspects of the day's events. Learn to critique yourself and learn from mistakes. Think about how other people may have perceived you on this day. Close your eyes and replay the events of the day in your mind's eye. Become your own mental coach.

37. Music as a tool

Purchase a Walkman or CD player for your office. Listen to classical and emotional music to stimulate your mind power. Use music as a motivational tool for your physical activities and watch your performance improve dramatically. When you drive home from work, or become stuck in traffic, play your favorite relaxing music to eliminate stress.

38. Become an early riser

No time of day is more silent and serene than early morning. Get up early and enjoy the sunset with your life-partner. Go for a walk through the woods before work to prepare your mind and stimulate clarity of purpose.

39. Think and act young

To stay in top physical condition and promote slow aging you must not let an old person move into your body and mind. Create a youthful and fun lifestyle that stimulates the mind and body. You are as old as you think and act. Enjoy tremendous vitality by living with zest, passion, and a youthful attitude.

40. Treat yourself

Allow yourself a rare treat every now and then to reward yourself. Buy something nice or have a delicious dessert once a week to celebrate your successes and accomplishments. Take a day off and do nothing except fun and interesting things that both you and your family enjoy.

41. Develop social skills and diplomacy

Stop and really listen to what people are saying and doing. Show your leadership through attentiveness and compassion. Take a stance on matters of importance, but learn to remain flexible.

Practice interacting with people of dissimilar likes and personalities to enhance your people skills.

42. Master patience

Every great person fails more times than he succeeds. Remember that persistence and patience breed success. Learn to pause and relax when you are feeling impatient and irritable. A great way to practice patience is to prepare a meal that takes a long time to cook when you are really hungry. When you are impatient or frustrated, walk away for a couple of minutes, then come back and tackle your task with renewed energy.

43. Encourage competition

Nothing motivates like competition. Develop the personal desire to be better than the next guy. Privately compete with your co-workers and exercise partner. The spirit of competition is what makes our society so amazingly productive and effective. Learn to compete against your previous performances and work success. Challenge success often and compete against poverty and illness.

44. Enjoy nature

Go on camping trips with your friends and family. Learn to rock or ice climb and challenge your fears. Surround yourself with plants at home and at work; if you can't go to nature, bring nature to you. Watch the Discovery channel or wildlife films with your children or spouse and enjoy the marvels of Mother Nature. Take up bird-watching or take a survival course and become proficient in back-woods navigation. Your children and grandchildren will forever be respectful of nature, if you take a stance and become concerned about the environment.

45. Take the path least traveled

Get into the habit of being original. Who says that you have to keep up with the Jonses? Find your own way and beliefs. Learn the concept of doing things the right way instead of the easy way. Stand for something and believe in it with integrity and honor.

46. Become physically competent

Accept the role of protector and defender of your spouse and family. Start taking lessons in boxing, martial arts, and self-defense. Don't go looking for fights, but be able to protect yourself and the ones you love. Feel the tremendous power and energy of physical competence in your life. Know when to act and when to walk away. There is nothing worth fighting for except your loved ones, but be prepared to do so.

47. Defeat your bad habits

We all have varying degrees of bad habits. Understand that you always pay consequences for bad habits sooner or later. Start reprogramming your mind to reduce and eliminate these from your life. Make a commitment and tell everyone about it; this will help in providing your motivation and support. Begin mastering self-discipline and open the doors to power living.

48. Become a traveler

A well-traveled person is a wise and worldly person. Pick a different country or destination each year and begin expanding your horizons. Take advantage of today's wonderful technology and travel abroad. Stay out of the tourist mode and start looking closer at life on this great planet.

49. Become an expert

Take a strong interest in any subject you like and learn all there is to know about it. Become studious and intimately knowledgeable about your business or profession. Write books and papers on your favorite subject and spend some time each day becoming an expert.

50. Master self-discipline

Understand that self-discipline is the solid foundation of all good actions and thoughts. Practice the techniques found in this book to enhance and stimulate the power of self-discipline. Become the person that people wish to emulate. Take the knowledge of power living and live powerfully.

51. Do nothing day

Set aside one day a week for doing absolutely nothing. Have no set schedule, no to-do list, no important phone calls, and only do what you like to do. It is very important to break the pattern of everyday life and allow yourself complete freedom to do what you want. Go see a movie or sleep in late.

52. Learn your opposites

If you are a man, learn how to cook, sew, and garden. If you are a woman, learn about vehicle maintenance, wood working, and lawn care. Stop limiting your knowledge because society has programmed you to accept certain skills and not others. Stop and think about what your opposite subjects and skills are, then begin expanding your knowledge base by learning.

53. I can / I can't

Start replacing the word I can't with the word I can. Reprogram your mind and attitude to accept no limits. The only reason you can't is because you are always telling yourself so. Begin changing your attitude by changing your thoughts and beliefs about what can and can't be accomplished. Start thinking like a super-human achiever.

54. The sixth sense

Start listening to that little voice of advice and intuition in the back of your mind. We all have the sixth sense, but you have to open your mind by exercising this powerful gut-feeling response. Use your sixth sense to solve problems and generate ideas. Pay attention to your gut-feelings, intuitions, unexplainable emotions, and that little voice.

55. Walk a mile

Don't be so quick to judge a person. Learn how to look past a person's attire, words, and personality. See him or her for what they truly are; one of God's creations. Before you pass judgement on somebody, you must first walk a mile in his or her shoes. Get in the habit of treating people with respect and courtesy, no matter what their status in society.

56. The weak inherit nothing

It may be true that the meek will inherit the Earth, but the law of nature says that the weak shall inherit nothing. super-humans are not frail, scared, or passive in their quest for success. Stick your chest out, look people square in the eyes, and begin gaining forward momentum in your life. The path of Power Living is above-average performance. Make a conscious effort to exhibit self-confidence and aggressive leadership abilities.

57. Power Breathing

Take a hint from ancient cultures and practice the art of deep breathing. Get into the habit of working your body to its maximum. Go farther and faster than you did the day before. Push yourself during physical exercise and condition your mind as well as your body.

58. Attitude of Resolve

Learn to break your comfort zone and welcome the challenges of life. Understand that hardship can build your resolve or make you a constant complainer. The attitude of resolve is body armor for your mind Start generating the powerful feeling of personal fortitude.

59. Take responsibility

Be as quick to take the blame, as you are to take credit. Understand that responsibility is the foundation of character and integrity. Stand up, be a strong man or be a proud woman, but most of all be responsible. Accept the responsibilities of leadership and be known for your compassion, integrity, and strength of character.

60. Priceless patience

When you feel yourself becoming impatient and anxious, take a deep breath and remember the virtue of patience. Learn to use patience as a powerful exercise for self-discipline. Force yourself to remain calm, cool, and collected when you are around children or in slow moving situations. Focus your attention to strengthening your patience, and you will defeat the symptoms of stress.

61. Never show weakness

Let your guard down with your loved ones and the people you truly trust. Don't allow your problems to effect your outward emotions at work or around unfamiliar people. In society, as in nature, showing weakness is a sure way of attracting predators. Learn to strengthen your resolve by controlling how you express your emotions.

62. Don't eat so much

Ever wonder why everybody seems to be fat and lethargic? It is because we eat more food than our stomachs were designed to hold. The typical American dinner would serve a family of five in most third-world countries. Learn to eat in moderation and stay away from all-you-can-eat buffets. Make the effort to eat six or seven small meals throughout the day, instead of three huge meals at set times.

63. Failure as medicine

Understand that failure is a fact of life. Don't expect to fail, but welcome failure as a teacher and it will enhance your wisdom. Start calling your problems "challenges", and use them as character builders and strategy planners. Be known as a person that never, ever gives up.

64. Develop character goals

Start setting daily and monthly character goals. Identify what character flaws you have and make a plan to improve them. Make each day a proving ground for character strength and every problem a personality challenge. Begin each day with a to-do list for your personal character development.

65. Practice concentration

Schedule time to clear your mind and practice mental focus skills. Sit quietly and observe the things around you. Focused concentration brings clarity of mind and serenity to our often crazy lives. Learn how to remove and ignore small distractions and experience the wonderful benefits of focused attention.

66. Endorphin fix

Start a cardiovascular exercise program that includes running or bicycling. Begin feeling a powerful surge of endorphins in your body when you vigorously exercise. The endorphin fix for the athlete is similar to the narcotic high that drug users feel, except that it is pure vitality, self-esteem, and health. Make the effort to get your heart and blood pumping on a daily basis, and reap the benefits of enhanced physical and mental performance.

67. Credit warfare

Credit cards and bad credit are two reasons why people struggle most of their adult lives. Become debt free and gain independence by cutting up your credit cards and paying cash for everything. Take the time to see what is on your credit report and begin building up solid credit. Don't allow big banks or financial institutions to stand in the way of your goals; begin treating your personal finances as a top priority.

68. Vitamin health

Take advantage of today's medical knowledge and yesterday's ancient longevity secrets, by supplementing your diet with vitamins and herbs. Become knowledgeable on the important subject of your body's vitamin and mineral needs. Make vitamin supplementation a part of your daily routine and experience a lifetime of vitality, energy, and enhanced health.

69. The power of suggestion

The subconscious mind is the most powerful aspect of the brain. Begin learning about the wonders and capabilities of your subconscious mind and the power of suggestion. Make it a daily habit to say your goals over and over in your mind. Give your subconscious mind positive suggestions and begin generating mental momentum.

70. The power of prayer

We all pray when things are at their worst or when we really want something, but get in the habit of praying to simply balance your spiritual life. Start praying for guidance, strength, and for the welfare of others. Use the power of prayer to open your mind and heart to discover your creator.

71. Power snacks

Get in the habit of bringing fruit, energy bars, and vegetables to work. Experience the benefits of healthy snacking and increased energy. Put down the candy bar and diet soda, and reach for an apple, carrot, or energy bar instead. Feel the difference that clean and healthy fuel makes in your physical motor.

72. Emotional control

Take the time to reflect upon your behavior. Ask your loved ones to critique how you control your emotional peaks and valleys. Make the conscious effort to recognize when your emotions are at an extreme, and practice the art of self-control.

73. Stand for something

Nobody likes a wishy-washy person. Believe in something and stand up for your opinions, but be careful to allow others the same courtesy. Take an interest in the environment, world affairs, politics, and join an organization that supports what you believe in. Stop complaining about the way things are and start doing something about it.

74. Experience the Internet

Use this amazing tool of technology to expand your horizons and knowledge base. Keep on top of your profession by learning how to use the limitless resources of the Internet. Technology is the foundation of our society's future, so make sure you are not left behind.

75. Become a listener

Make the conscious effort to keep quiet and truly listen to your loved ones and co-workers. Stop offering advice and suggestions, simply close your mouth and become a good listener. Improve your relationship and marriage by truly being interested in what your significant other has to say.

76. Advance in the direction of your dreams

Do something each day to help bring you closer to achieving your goals. Turn off the television and spend one hour each day accomplishing a goal-related task. Make it a priority to talk often with your spouse about your strategy and goal progress.

77. The value of preparation

We all know that poor planning will result in poor performance. Make sure that you are well prepared for the day ahead before retiring for the evening. Devote 30 minutes each evening for preparation to ensure that your early mornings are as stress-free and relaxed as possible. Take the time to set out your clothing, organize your briefcase, prepare a lunch, and develop a to-do list before going to bed.

78. Charisma

Work on developing a charismatic personality. Practice the art of socializing and public speaking. Make it a point to be interested in what other people are saying. Learn to smile more and memorize a few light jokes to encourage conversation. Work on your charisma and you will develop the ability to interact with difficult people in difficult situations.

79. Stay informed

Make it a point to stay on top of current events and new developments. Get into the habit of reading several different newspapers each day. Subscribe to magazines that cover world affairs, technology, health, and finance. Remember that knowledge is power.

80. Have a mentor

Learn how to take solid advice from successful and happy people. Have a mentor that offers advice in a time of need. Make it a priority to learn from the mistakes of others. Keep control of your ego and practice the skill of being humble. Remember that having money is not always a reflection of intelligence or wisdom.

81. Nature bound

Take the time to get out of your office and into nature. Set aside leisure time to walk in the park, or go camping in the mountains. Nature has a way of putting things in perspective for you. Get back in touch with your humanity by letting nature show you how small your problems really are.

82. Organize your life

Take the time to clean, maintain, and organize your house and possessions. Schedule one day every two weeks for organizational tasks. Find the discipline to organize those areas of your life that always seem to be in disarray. Increase your productivity and efficiency by organizing your goals, possessions, and time.

83. To do list

Most people have tried a to-do list, but few people ever follow through with it. Start incorporating a to-do list into your life. Make it a priority to accomplish everything on your list. Begin by starting small and simple, then add more detailed items over time. All organized and efficient achievers use to-do lists as a powerful work tool.

84. Water for life

Your body is approximately 70% water. Most people never drink the required eight glasses a day, and their mental and physical performance suffers. Make it a point to drink water instead of coffee and start benefitting from a well-hydrated system. Always have a source of water readily available to you at home and at work.

85. Be early

Make it a habit of always being 10 to 15 minutes early for every appointment. Set your watch 10 minutes ahead and you will always be early. Show your discipline and motivation by being well prepared for your appointments.

86. Identify habits

We all possess particular habits and traits that are annoying to others or harmful to ourselves. Take the time to critique your personal habits, both good and bad. Make a list of what you want and need to change about yourself. Begin using self-discipline to defeat these habits. Remember that nobody is perfect, but some people come close.

87. Nutritional warfare

Take the time to learn about the poisons and toxins stacked on every shelf in every supermarket. Make it a point to only eat pure and clean foods. Become an expert on the fuel that your body requires. Remember that you truly are what you eat, and nutrition is the key to health and vitality.

88. Hard times

It doesn't matter how many problems you have, somebody will always have more. Stop and take a hard look at how blessed you really are, and ask yourself if these are truly hard times. In this day and age, we have forgotten what real struggle and survival is all about. Take the time to talk to an older person that lived during the Great Depression and see if you really know what hard times mean. Be thankful for all that you have every day of the year.

89. I was wrong

These three simple words are the most difficult in the English language to say. Become a better husband, wife, and human being by admitting when you are wrong, and even sometimes when you're not. Make sure your ego does not outweigh your common sense and ability to be humble.

90. Power room

Have a special place in your home or office where you can go for peace and quiet reflection. Make a power room that offers you privacy for meditation and peaceful reflection. Have quiet music and pictures of your goals on the wall. Use this place as a base for motivation and serenity.

91. Challenge your mind

Stop vegetating in front of the television or home computer. Start challenging your mind with crossword puzzles, word games, sports, chess, and by learning new skills. Remember that you cannot afford to allow your brain to remain inactive, so get up and get thinking. Make it a point to learn something new each day. Challenge your mind and open the door to your creative genius.

92. Inspiration

Read motivational and inspirational books. Make self-improvement a top priority in your life by reading inspirational stories of human accomplishment and success. Begin to learn how others have joined the ranks of the high-achievers and find motivation in these stories. Start stocking your personal library with books on success and self-improvement, and generate new ideas from the world's most successful people.

93. Worry wart

Stop allowing every little problem and situation eat up so much of your thinking. Begin laughing out loud when you feel yourself worrying about something. Get in the habit of defeating thoughts that worry you and regain your never-say-die attitude.

94. Man's Jail

Nothing can bring down a man or woman faster than desire. Learn to harness the power of self-control and stay away from instant gratification. Your success as a human being is directly related to your ability to control desire and develop strong personal discipline.

95. Chivalry and integrity

The monks of Tibet practice the philosophy of building personal integrity and practicing human chivalry every day of their lives. Character is the defining critique of your personality, strength, weakness, and personal integrity. Learn to place top priority on human chivalry and personal integrity.

96. Green power

Surround your home and work space with beautiful life-giving plants. Use nature's oxygen factory to improve your health and emotional well being. Plants calm the mind and create an atmosphere of relaxation. Begin learning about plant life and ancient herbal medicine by adding several herbal plants to your home or office. The added responsibility of caring for several plants is an excellent way to exercise and build self-discipline.

97. Golden silence

An ancient Far East technique for building discipline and mental focus is to observe one half-hour of total silence each day. Sit in your office or home and concentrate on the beauty of silence. Do no physical or mental activity except to think about your goals and self-improvement. Use the power of silence to reflect and meditate upon your performance as a human being, and how you can improve each area of your life. Let other people know that you wish not to be disturbed during this time and begin experiencing the wonders of reflection and silence.

98. The look of discipline

Your appearance should not be dictated by the current fad, fashion, or style. Keep your hair short and neat, your clothes pressed and starched, and your extremities well groomed. Maintain the look of a disciplined human being by spending extra time and effort on a no-nonsense appearance. Learn how to shine your shoes and wear dark blue or black business attire at all times. Remember that you are a leader who sets the standard of excellence for all to see, and not a sheep who follows the fads and fashions of the sheep herd.

99. *Good Karma / Bad Karma*

Do good things and give more of yourself than you take, and you will begin experiencing the power of personal Karma. Understand that all bad and unjust actions will come back on you ten-times stronger. Make charity a monthly habit, and give a little of your good fortune back to the world. Remember the age-old saying of "you reap what you sow", and understand that integrity, honor, and strong moral character generate your good Karma.

100. *Goal warrior*

Begin setting daily, monthly, yearly, and lifelong goals for yourself. Attack your goals and desires like a commando, but use common sense and moderation when setting them. Get accustomed to writing down your goals and keep a journal of your progress and efforts. Understand that goals provide motivation, persistence, satisfaction, and emotional well being. You must begin writing down your goals this very minute, or drift aimlessly through life without direction.

POWER LIVING CONCLUSION

As a student of self-discipline, you have been exposed to the finest techniques and knowledge from some of the world's most successful people and Special Operations Units. Go back and slowly read this book from time to time, and allow the information to become ingrained in your mind. The concept of power living is one of taking direct action to enhance the quality of our short existence on this great planet.

Think of today as a new beginning in your life. Do something, anything, to correct that which is wrong with your daily performance. Every day do something that will enhance your happiness, health, wealth, and vitality. Life is too short to just sit around and wait for something to happen. When you begin to think that you have it so hard, or life is not fair, stop and take a look around you to see things as they truly are. Don't accept average or normal, leave a legacy of success and honor behind. Complaining is the mark of a loser, and action is the badge of a winner. I don't expect you to completely change your life around, but make a small change for the better. I wish you luck and health!

Stop complaining, get up, get out, and begin power living!!!

BIBLIOGRAPHY / RECOMMENDED READING

SELF-DISCIPLINE

DISCIPLINE –The Glad Surrender, by Elisabeth Elliot
Baker Books Publishing: 1982. This wonderful Christian
book covers the topics of discipline, commitment, and
integrity.

THE MASTER-KEY TO RICHES, by Napoleon Hill
Ballantine Publishing Group: 1965. Truly one of the greatest
books of all time. Napoleon Hill covers self-discipline and
successful strategies of the world's most noted people.

A BETTER WAY TO LIVE, by Og Mandino
Bantam Books Publishing: 1990. A personal guide to
developing self-discipline and the skills to live a fulfilling
life.

THE TIBETAN BOOK OF LIVING AND DYING, by
Sogyal Rinpoche
Harper Collins Publishing: 1993. A comprehensive look at
the philosophies and teachings of the Tibetan monks.

MINDSCIENCE, by The Dalai Lama,
Wisdom Publishing: 1991. A direct look at ancient wisdoms
and modern truths.

DIALOGUES WITH SCIENTISTS AND SAGES, by Renee
Weber
Routledge Publishing: 1986. A comparison between modern
scientific research and ancient philosophies.

PERSONHOOD- The Art of Being Fully Human, by Leo F. Buscaglia
Ballantine Books Publishing: 1978. A refreshing look at understanding our individual journey through life.

THE WAY OF ZEN, by A. Watts
Random House, Inc: 1974. A mystical approach to understanding life.

THE CRACK IN THE COSMIC EGG, by J. Pierce
Julian Press, Inc: 1971. One of the most touching books on searching for meaning in life.

BLACK ELK SPEAKS, by John G. Neihardt
University of Nebraska Press: 1979. Insights from one of the greatest American Indian thinkers.

HOW TO STOP WORRYING AND START LIVING, by Dale Carnegie
Pocket Books: 1985. A masterful book for dealing with life.

THE POWER OF YOUR SUBCONSCIOUS MIND, by Dr. Joseph Murphy
Bantam Books: 1982. The most in-depth guide to understanding and using the power of the subconscious mind.

GROW RICH WITH PEACE OF MIND, by Napoleon Hill
Ballantine Books: 1964. Another great book on mental discipline and success.

ZEN IN THE MARTIAL ARTS, by Joe Hyams
Bantam Books: 1982. A pocket guide to discipline.

THE TOA OF LEADERSHIP, by John Heider
Bantam Books: 1984. Philosophies and ancient leadership styles.

PERSONAL ACHIEVEMENT

HOW TO SUCCEED- Dynamic Mind Principles, by Brian Adams
Wilshire Book Company: 1985. An excellent book on the science of success.

ADVANCED FORMULA FOR TOTAL SUCCESS, by Dr. Robert Anthony
Berkley Publishing: 1988. A user-friendly guide for better living.

THE 7 HABITS OF HIGHLY EFFECTIVE PEOPLE, by Steven R. Covey
Simon & Schuster: 1994. A must-read book for anyone interested in improving their life.

YOUR SUBCONSCIOUS POWER, by Charles M. Simmons
Wilshire Book Company: 1965. The most comprehensive book on using your subconscious for success.

THE MILLIONAIRE NEXT DOOR, by Thomas Stanley & William Danko
Pocket Books: 1996. A complete guide to understanding the reality behind the science of wealth.

SUCCESS IS A CHOICE, by Rick Pitino
Broadway Books: 1998. This book examines the road to success in both the athletic arena and everyday life.

THE DYNAMIC LAWS OF PROSPERITY, by Catherine Ponder
Prentice-Hall Publishing: 1962. A great mix of Christianity and the journey towards personal success.

HOW HIGH CAN YOU BOUNCE?, by Roger Crawford
Bantam Books: 1998. An inspiring book to help you get over
the hard times in life.

10001 WAYS TO ENERGIZE EMPLOYEES, by Bob
Nelson
Workman Publishing: 1997. The complete guide of ideas for
inspiring people in the workplace.

THINK AND GROW RICH, by Napoleon Hill
Ballantine Books: 1960. Truly the greatest book ever written
on personal achievement.

THE GREATEST MYSTERY IN THE WORLD, by Og
Mandino
Ballantine Publishing Group: 1997. An inspiring tale of self-
motivation and personal discovery.

SUCCESS THROUGH A POSITIVE MENTAL
ATTITUDE, by Napoleon Hill. Pocket Books: 1960.
Discover the mental science behind acquiring a winning
attitude.

DEBT-FREE LIVING, by Larry Burkett
Moody Press: 1989. A spiritual success guide for controlling
your finances.

THE BIBLE, by God and his disciples
Countless Publishers: The single most important book ever
written.

GET A FINANCIAL LIFE, by Beth Kobliner
Simon & Schuster: 1996. The complete guide to finances in
the 90's.

THE POWER OF POSITIVE THINKING, by Norman
Vincent Peale
Prentice-Hall: 1958. The most complete work on mental
success in print.

THE MAGIC OF BELIEVING, by Claude M. Bristol
Prentice-Hall: 1955. A powerful lesson in personal faith.

MIND AND BODY

A BRIEF HISTORY OF TIME, by Steven W. Hawking
Bantam Books: 1988. A unique and intelligent philosophy on
life.

THINKING BODY, DANCING MIND, by Chungliang Al
Huang and Jerry Lynch
Bantam Books: 1992. The Tao of performance in athletics
and life.

RAJA YOGA, by Wallace Slater
Theosophical Publishing House: 1968. A complete guide to
mental and physical well-being.

FIT FOR LIFE, by Harvey and Marilyn Diamond
Bantam Books: 1987. Sound advice for healthy living.

DR. WHITAKER'S GUIDE TO NATURAL HEALING, by
Julian Walker
Prima Publishing: 1995. An intelligent look at total health.

MUSCLES ALIVE, by J.V. Basmajian
Williams & Wilkins Company: 1979. All you ever wanted to
know about your body.

SEVEN ARROWS, by Hyemeyohsts Storm
Ballantine Books: 1972. An American Indian philosophy
book for life.

POWER READING, by Laurie Rozakis
Simon & Schuster: 1995. A comprehensive guide to better
reading skills.

12 STEPS TO BETTER MEMORY, by Carol Turkington
Simon & Schuster: 1996. The science of improved memory.

SCHOLAR WARRIOR, by Deng Ming-Dao
Harper-Collins: 1990. The development of Tao for everyday
life.

LOVE, DEATH & EXILE, by Bassam K. Frangieh
Georgetown University Press: 1990. Poems of inspiration.

STOP SCREAMING AT THE MICROWAVE, by Mary
Loverde
Simon & Schuster: 1998. A unique guide to life-
management.

THE SAYINGS OF THE VIKINGS, by Bjorn Jonasson
Gudrun Publishing: 1992. Hardy advice from the warrior
society.

THE EINSTEIN FACTOR, by Win Wenger & Richard Poe
Prima Publishing: 1995. A unique look at boosting your
intelligence.

PSYCHO-CYBERNETICS, by Maxwell Maltz
Prentice-Hall: 1960. A fascinating look at our mental
possibilities.

QUOTATIONARY, by Leonard Roy Frank
Random House: 1999. Over 20,000 quotations for life.

SPORTS SUPPLEMENT REVIEW, by Bill Phillips
Mile High Publishing: 1999. The most complete guide to
nutrition that you can find.

BUS 9 TO PARADISE, by Leo F. Buscaglia
Ballantine Books: 1977. A fascinating look at our lives in
progress.

HOW TO ARGUE AND WIN EVERYTIME, by Gerry
Spence
St. Martin's Press: 1995. The best information on persuasion.

APPENDICES

OGRANIZATIONS & INFORMATION SOURCES

Special Operations Consulting
1005 Banyan Drive, Virginia Beach, VA 23462. Attn: Michael A. Janke; (757) 560 – 3701 or www.specopsconsulting.com
    SOC is a professional consulting service that specializes in keynote speeches, presentations, books, tapes, and corporate consulting. Their expertise covers improving personal and professional performance, leadership, teamwork, and management training. They also work hand-in-hand with meeting planners, corporations, and individuals to customize presentations and training sessions to meet any need. (Founded by the author of this book.)

C.D. Lilly, Inc.
24195 Jaunita Drive, Quail Valley, CA 92587 Attn: Deborah Lilly; (800) 543 - 2360 or www.cdlilly.com
    C.D. Lilly, Inc. is a full-service speaking bureau that specializes in providing high-performance speakers for all occasions, as well as providing customized services for professional speakers.

Antion & Associates
http://www.antion.com / E-mail: tomantion@aol.com

Leading Authorities, Inc.
919 18th street, N.W. Suite 500
Wash, D.C. 20006 (202) 783-0300

The Speakers Bureau
P.O. Box 390296
Minneapolis, MN 55439-0296 (800) 397-2841

The Jack Morton Company
1725 K Street Nw, Suite 1400 (202) 296-1783
Washington, DC 20006

SELF-HELP, BUSINESS, AND MENTAL HEALTH ASSOC.

National Speakers Association
1500 South Priest Drive
Tempe, AZ 85281-6203
Phone: (602) 968-2552
Fax: 1-(602) 968-0911

**Meeting Planers Int'l
Northern California Chapter**
74 New Montgomery Suite 230
San Francisco, CA 94105
Phone: (415) 896-6447
URL: http://www.nccmpi.org

**Trade Show Exhibitors
Association**
5501 Backlick Road Suite 105
Springfield, VA 22151
Phone: (703) 941-3725

**Professional Convention
Management Association**
100 Vestavia Parkway
Suite 220
Birmingham, AL 35216-3743
Phone: (205) 823-7262

**American Diabetes
Association**
1701 N. Beauregard St
Alexandria, VA 22311
Phone: (703) 549-1500

American Lung Association
1740 Broadway
New York, NY 10019
Phone: (212) 315-8700
Fax: 1-(212) 315-6498
URL: http://www.nsbu.org

**Meeting Professionals &
Associates**
11021 SE 64th Street
Renton, WA 98056
Phone: (206) 226-1727

**American Marketing
Association**
31 South Wacker Drive
Suite 5800
Chicago, IL 60606
Phone: (312) 542-9000
URL: http://www.ama.org/

**Marketing Research
Association**
1344 Silas Deane Hwy
Suite 306
Rocky Hill, CT 06067-0230
Phone: (860) 257-4008
URL: http://www.mra-net.org/

Internet Business Alliance
PO Box 11518
Seattle, WA 98110
URL: http://www.alliance.org
Phone: (206) 780-2245

**National Association of
Alcoholism
and Drug Abuse Counselors**
1911 North Fort Meyer Drive
Suite #900 Arlington, VA
22209
Phone: (703) 741-7686
URL: http://www.naadac.org

**National Small Business
United**
1156 15th Street N.W.
Suite 710
Washington, DC 20005
Phone: (202) 293-8830

**National Association of
Private
Enterprise**
7819 Shelburn Circle
San Francisco, CA 94105-2411
Phone: (415) 764-4942
Dallas, TX 77379
Phone: (800) 223-6273
URL: http://www.nape.org

**National Association for the
Self-Employed**
1023 15th ST
Washington, DC 2005-2600
Phone: (202) 466-2100
URL: http://www.nase.org

**National Association of Home
Based Businesses**
10451 Mill Run Circle
Owings Mills, MD 21117
Phone: (410) 363-3698
http://www.usahomebusiness.co
m/expan.htm

**American Psychiatric
Association**
1400 K. St., N.W.
Washington, DC 20005
Phone: (202) 682-6000
URL: http://www.psych.org/

**Northern California Society
American Society of
Association Executives**
74 Montgomery Suite 230
Washington, DC 20005-1168
Phone: (202) 626-2723
Fax: 1-(202) 371-8825

**The National Foundation of
Women Business Owners**
1100 Wayne Ave
Suite 830
Silver Springs, MD 20910
Phone: (301) 608-2590
URL: http://www.nawbo.org

**National Women's Business
Council**
409 Third Street SW
Washington, DC 20024
Phone: (202) 205-3850
URL: http:
/www.womenconnect.com/nwb

**Center for Mental Health
Services**
P.O. Box 42490
Washington, DC 20015
1-800-789-CMHS (2647)
URL:
http://www.mentalhealth.org/
URL:http://www.ncsae.org

**American Psychological
Association**
750 First Street, NE,
Washington, D.C.20002-4242
Phone (202) 336-5500
URL: http://www.apa.org/

**National Mental Health
Association**
1021 Prince Street
Alexandria, VA 22314-2971
Phone (703) 684-7722
or (800) 969-nmha

**Families Worldwide
International**
Families Worldwide
75 East Fort Union Blvd.
Salt Lake City, UT 84047 USA
Phone: USA (801) 562-6178
URL:
http://www.fww.org/index.html

**American Psychoanalytic
Association**
309 East 49th Street
New York, New York 10017
Phone (212) 593-0571
URL: http://www.apsa.org

**The Retired Officers
Association**
201 North Washington Street
Alexandria, VA 22314
Phone: 703-838-0546
URL: http://www.troa.org

**Substance Abuse and Mental
Health
Services Administration**
Room 12-105 Parklawn
Building
5600 Fishers Lane
Rockville, MD 20857
301-443-4795 or 301-443-0284
URL: http://www.samhsa.gov/

**American Academy of Child
and Adolescent Psychiatry**
P.O. Box 96106,
Washington, D.C. 20090-6106
Phone: (202) 966-7300

SelfGrowth.com
96 Linwood Plaza
Suite 264
Fort Lee, NJ 07024
201-945-6757
fax: (201) 945-7441
URL:
http://www.selfgrowth.com

**American Society of
Addiction Medicine**
4601 North Park Avenue
Arcade Suite 101
Chevy Chase, MD 20815
Phone: 301-656-3920

**Alliance for Children and
Families**
11700 West Lake Park Drive
Milwaukee, WI 53224
Phone: 800-221-3726 Ext: 3689

**Summit Consulting Group,
Inc.**
Box 1009 East Greewich, RI
02818
Contact: Alan Weiss, Ph.D.
Phone: 800-766-7935

National Assoc. of Women
Business Owners
1100 Wayne Ave Suite 830
Silver Springs, MD 20910
Phone: (301) 608-2590

The Institute for Global Ethics
11 Main Street
PO Box 563
Camden, ME 04843
Phone: 800-729-2615

AACN
American Assoc. of Critical Care Nurses
101 Columbia,
Aliso Viejo, CA 92656-1491
Phone: 1-800-899-2226
URL: http://www.aacn.org

Christian Medical & Dental Society
P.O. Box 7500
501 Fifth Street
Bristol, TN 37621-7500
Phone: 423-844-1000

American Society for Reproductive Medicine
409 12th Street, SW Suite 203
Washington, DC 20024-2125
Phone: 202-863-2439

American Legion National Headquarters
700 N. Pennsylvania Street
Indianapolis, IN 46204
Phone: (317) 630-1200

American Social Health Association
PO Box 13827
Research Triangle Park, NC 27709
Phone: 919-361-8416

WEBSITES AND E-ZINES

SUCCESS, SELF-HELP, AND PERSONAL ACHIEVEMENT WEBSITES

http://www.achievement.com
http://www.celestialvisions.com
http://www.home.hiwaay.net
http://www.anthonygalie.com
http://www.attitudeiseverything.com
http://www.au.spiritweb.org
http://www.wcbagency-tm.com/WBT.htm
http://www.tracyint.com
http://www.carmine.net
http://www.dale-carnegie.com
http://www.mindtools.com/lifeplan.html
http://www.selfgrowth.com
http://www.walters-intl.com
http://www.franklincovey.com/priorities
http://www.ahandyguide.com/cat1
http://www.selfhelp.com/bootstraps.html
http://www.rockisland.com/~process/millenniumk
http://www.thinkright.offc.com
http://www.onlineconsulting.com
http://www.sanspareil.com/
http://www.is17.com/promo/reports
http://www.success.com/
http://www.geocities.com/Athens/Oracle/3007
http://www.cdipage.com
http://www.mentalfitness.com/
http://www.rocketreader.com

http://www.gen.com
http://www.barronspecialties.com
http://webagency-tm.com
http://www.tiac.net
http://www.mindmedia.com
http://www.botree.com/index.htm
http://www.newage.com/
http://www.newfrontier.com/
http://www.inner-resources.com/success/
http://www.yogajournal.com/
http://www.mentalhelp.net/psyhelp/
http://www.grayarea.com/gray2.htm
http://www.metamorphosis-online.com/self_improvement/self_help.htm
http://www.innercite.com
http://www.au.spiritweb.org
http://www.netstoreusa.com
http://www.celestialvisions.com
http://www.telusplanet.net
http://www.megavision.net
http://www.family.com/
http://www.success-motivation.com
http://www.instant-success.com/
http://www.linktosuccess.com/
http://www.mentalhelp.net
http://www.psych-central.com
http://www.menatlhealth.com
http://www.tbm.org
http://www.depression.com

INTERNET RESOURCES A - Z

ADDICTIONS

12 Step Cyber Café
www.12steps.org
3D Prevention Coalition
www.3dmonth.org
Addiction Treatment Forum
www.atforum.com
Alternatives in Treatment
www.drughelp.com
Betty Ford Center
www.bettyfordcenter.org
Join Together
www.jointogether.org
National Counsel
www.nationalcounseling.com
Nicorette www.nicorette.com
Physicians for Prevention
www.pfprevention.com
Serenity Lane
www.serenitylane.org
Teen Challenge
www.teenchallenge.com

ADVICE

Dr. Laura www.drlaura.com
Dr. Paula www.drpaula.com
Quick Advice
www.quickadvice.com
The Right Answer
www.therightanswer.com

ALTERNATIVE MEDICINE

Alternative Therapists
www.asat.org

American Holistic Health
Association www.ahha.org
Ayurvedia Center
www.ayurvedahc.com
Ayurvedic Institute
www.ayur.com
Cosmic Breath
www.thecosmicbreath.com
Health Pyramid
www.healthpyramid.com
Holistic Internet Resources
www.hir.com
Holistic Living Magazine
www.holisticliving.org
Homeopaths
www.homeopathy.org
Natural Health
www.naturalhealth.org
Your Life - Your Choice
www.Life-Choices.com
Positive Pathways
www.positivepathways.com

BOOK RESOURCES

21st Century Christian
Bookstore www.21stcc.com
A1 Books www.a1books.com
Amazon www.amazon.com
Barnes & Noble
www.barnesandnoble.com
Best Books
www.bestbooks.com
Book Buyers
www.bookbuyers.com
Book Express
www.bookexpress.com
Book of the Month
www.enlishbooks.com
Book Port www.bookport.com

Book Stacks www.books.com
Book Watch
www.bookwatch.com
Book Zen www.bookzen.com
Book Wire www.bookwire.com
Book World
www.bookworld.com
Book Zone www.bookzone.com
Books Online
www.booksonline.com
Borders www.borders.com
Corporate Book Service
www.cidsource.com
Just Good Books
www.justgoodbooks.com
Olsson's Books
www.olssons.com
Papyrus Books
www.papyrusbooks.com
Readers Ndex
www.readersndex.com
Specialty Books
www.specialty-books.com
Super Library
www.superlibrary.com
United States Book Exchange
www.usbe.com

BUSINESS JOURNALS

Business Journals
www.amcity.com
Business Publications
Association www.bizpubs.org
Industry Week
www.industryweek.com

EXPERTS

Find A Professional
www.findaprofessional.com
Experts www.experts.com
Experts Exchange
www.experts-exchange.com

ELECTRONIC COMMERCE

Internet Marketing Tips
www.marketingtips.com
E-Marketer
www.emarketer.com
EC Today www.ectoday.com
All E-Commerce
www.allec.com
Electronic Markets
www.electronicmarkets.com

FITNESS

24 Hour Fitness
www.24hourfitness.com
Aerobics and Fitness
www.afaa.com
All About Fitness
www.allaboutfitness.com
Alliance for Health
www.aahperd.org
Athletic Trainers Association
www.nata.org
Balance Fitness
www.balance.net
Cardiovascular Institute
www.cardio.com
Cybercise www.cybercise.com
Exercise Council
www.acefitness.org
Fit @ Home
www.fitahome.com
Fit Net www.fit-net.com
Fit Online www.fitonline.com
Fit Org www.fit.org
Fitness Health & Weight Loss
www.landry.com
Fitness News Online Health &
Fitness Mag.
www.fitnessnews.com
Fitness Professionals
www.aahfp.com

Fitness World
www.fitnessworld.com
Men's Fitness
www.mensfitness.com
National Gym Association
www.nationalgym.com
Physical Fitness
www.physical.com
World Fitness
www.worldfitness.org

HEALTH

America's Health Network
www.ahn.com
Acupuncture
www.acupuncture.com
American Medical Association
www.ama-assn.org
American Heart Association
www.amhrt.org
Ask The Doc www.ask-the-doc.com
Better Health
www.betterhealth.com
British Medical Journal
www.bmj.com
Caregiving Newsletter
www.caregiving.com
Health A to Z
www.healthatoz.com
Health Connection
www.healthconnection.com
Health Guide
www.healthguide.com
Health Information Center
www.nhic-nt.health.org
Health Library www.health-library.com
Health World
www.healthy.com
Life lines www.lifelines.com
Medical Center
www.medcenter.com

Men's Health
www.menshealth.com

MARRIAGE

Center for Growth
www.acenter4growth.com
Marriage Alive
www.marriagealive.com
Marriage Encounter
www.encounter.org
Marriage Help
www.episcopalme.com
Marriage Toolbox
www.marriagetools.com
National Marriage Encounter
www.marriages.com

MENTAL HEALTH

British Psychotherapists
www.bcp.org.uk
Counselor Link
www.counselorlink.com
Cyber Couch
www.cybercouch.com
In Stream Psychlink
www.psychlink.com
Liberation Psychotherapy
www.liberationpsych.org
Lynn Mental Health
Association www.glmh.org
Mediation www.osho.org
Mental Health
www.mentalhealth.com
Mental Health Net
www.mentalhelp.net
Psychological Advisor
www.psynews.com
Re-evaluation Counseling
www.rc.org
Save www.save.org
Shyness www.shyness.com

Therapeutic Camps
www.natwc.org

MILITARY

Air Force www.af.mil
Air Force Association
www.afa.org
Air National Guard
www.ang.af.mil
American Legion
www.legion.org
Armed Forces Association
www.uafa.org
Army Corps of Engineers
www.usace.army.mil
Army Times
www.armytimes.com
Civil Air Patrol www.cap.af.mil
Coast Guard R&D
www.rdc.uscg.mil
Defense News
www.defensenews.com
Department of the Navy
www.tql-navy.org
Department of Veteran Affairs
www.va.gov
Marine Corps Association
www.mca-marines.org
Marine Link www.usmc.mil
Militaria Magazine
www.militaria.com
Military Career Guide
www.militarycareers.com
Military City
www.militarycity.com
Military Network
www.military-network.com
National Guard Association
www.ngaus.org
Navy Seals
www.navyseals.com
Special Forces Association
www.sfahq.org

U.S. Army Association
www.ausa.org
Veterans News www.vnis.com
Veterans www.vets.com

NEWSLETTERS

Bizy Moms
www.bizymoms.com
Circles of Light
www.circlesoflight.com
Global Net News
www.dalepublishing.com
Great Speaking
www.antion.com
Marketing Tools
www.MarketingToolz.com
Mind Matters
www.hypnosis.org
New Ideas www.mgeneral.com
Parenting Thoughts
www.ParentingToolbox.com
Poor Richards
www.PoorRichards.com
The Symposium
www.selfknowledge.org
Weekly Web News Clips
www.zazz.com
Women's entrepreneur Network
www.weon.com

PARENTING

Child Development Institute
www.cdipage.com
Common Sense Parenting
www.parenting.com
Cyber Mom
www.thecybermom.com
Daddys Home
www.daddyshome.com
Dads Can www.dadscan.org
Family Network
www.familnetwork.com

Family Resource
www.familyresource.com
Father Project
www.fatherproject.com
Fatherhood Initiative
www.fatherhood.org
Fathering www.fathering.org
Fathering Magazine
www.fatheringmag.com
Fathers Net
www.fathersnetwork.org
Fathers of America
www.ufa.org
Informed Parent
www.informedparent.com
Help for Families
www.helpforfamilies.com
Moms www.momsonline.com
Moms Net
www.momsnetwork.com
Parent Info Net www.npin.org
Parenting Press
www.parentingpress.com
Parents Talk www.parents-talk.com
Positive Parenting
www.positiveparenting.com
Whole Family Center
www.wholefamily.com

PHILOSOPHY

Anthroposophic Press
www.anthropress.org
Catholic Philosophial
Association www.acpa-main.org
Confucius Publishing
www.confuscius.org
Electric Minds www.minds.com
Fellowship of Reason
www.kindreason.com
Human Condition
www.condition.org
Life Force News
www.haribol.org
Pearls of Wisdom
www.pearls.org

VETERANS

American Legion
www.legion.org
American Gulf War Veterans
www.gulfwarvets.com
Catholic War Veterans
www.ocwvets.org
Families Alliance
www.nationalalliance.org
Merchant Marines
www.usmm.org
National Veterans Organization
www.nvo.org
Retired Officers Association
www.troa.org
Submarine Vets www.ussvi.org
VFW www.vfw.org
Veterans Observer
www.theveteransobserver.com
Viet Nam Veterans
www.vietvet.org
Veterans Voice www.vvoa.com

PERSONAL ACHIEVEMENT MAGAZINES & JOURNALS

SUCCESS MAGAZINE
P.O. Box 3038, Harlan, IA 51537. 1-800-234-7324
A top-notch magazine for information about personal success and up-to-date corporate strategies.

PRIORITIES MAGAZINE – The Journal of Personal and Professional Success
2200 West Parkway Blvd., Salt Lake City, UT 84119. 1-800-236-2569
One of the most interesting and informative magazines available. If you are interested in the latest information and strategies on personal achievement, this is your best bet. Published by the Franklin Covey Corporation. (formed by well-known author and achievement Guru –Stephen R. Covey).

PSYCHOLOGY TODAY
49 East 21st Street, 11th Floor, NYC, NY 10010. 1-800-234-8361
To stay up on the latest developments in the world of psychology and mental health, this is the where the experts go. Packed full of helpful information for daily life and personal improvement.

SPARE TIME – The Magazine of Money-Making Opportunities
2400 S.Commerce Drive, Suite 400, New Berlin, WI 53151 (262)-780-1070
A great magazine for the latest strategies and opportunities in today's business arena. Offers excellent information and resources for small to medium businesses.
www.spare-time.com (one of the best small business websites available)

NEW MAN MAGAZINE

600 Rinehart Rd. Lake Mary, Florida 32746 (407) 333-0600
    For character building, achievement, and Christian-based information. A very informative magazine for all areas of life. Offers excellent personal and spiritual success resources. http://www.newmanmag.com

SMART MONEY

1755 Broadway, New York, NY 10019 (212) 765-7323
    One of the best money, investment, and wealth-building information sources available. Find personal financial resources and information in every article.

FORTUNE

Time & Life Building, Rockefeller Center, New York, NY 10020 Fax (212) 522-7686/ E-mail: fortune-letters@pathfinder.com ,Url: http://www.fortune.com
    Another personal success and finance powerhouse. This magazine covers all aspects of business, retirement, and Wall Street strategies for success.

WRITERS' JOURNAL- The Complete Writer's Magazine

P.O Box 394, Perham, MN 56573-0394 (218) 346-7921/ E-mail: writersjournal@wadena.net, Url: http://www.sowashco.com/writersjournal/
    An excellent source for putting your thoughts into words. Keep up on the latest tools and techniques for successful writing, publishing, and promoting.

ENTREPRENEUR – The Small Business Authority

12 W. 31st St, #1100, New York, NY 10001 (212) 563-8080, Url: http://www.entrepreneurmag.com
    This magazine is truly the small business authority. To keep up on the latest trends and information in the world of small business, this is the magazine.

INC. - The Magazine for Growing Companies
38 Commercial Wharf, Boston, MA 02110 (617) 248-8000/ E-mail: editors@inc.com, Url: http://www.inc.com
For anyone looking to increase their financial standing or business sense, this magazine covers all aspects of business and financial success.

FAST COMPANY
77 North Washington St, Boston, MA 02114-1927 (800) 688-1545, E-mail: loop@fastcompany.com / Url: http://www.fastcompany.com
A hip new technological magazine for everything you ever wanted to know about the Internet market place. Packed full of success stories and advice from those who are making it work on the Internet.

BONKERS? - A Magazine for Our Times
333 Royal Poinciana Plaza, P.O. Box 189 Palm Beach, FL 33480 (800) 403-8850 E-mail: bonkers@goingbonkers.com / Url: www.goingbonkers.com
A truly unique self-help magazine. Loaded with wonderful stories and articles about personal development, stress-free living, and every day life.

ALTERNATIVE MEDICINE
21 ½ Main St Tiburon, GA 94920 (604) 664-7455 E-mail: jeff@dotcom.bc.ca / Url:http://www.alternativemedicine.com
A first-rate alternative heath magazine that provides helpful ideas, products, and articles on improving your health naturally.

MUSCLE & FITNESS
P.O Box 37208 Boone, IA 50037-2208 (800) 998-0731 Url: http:www.muscle-fitness.com
For the development of physical discipline and health, this is the most comprehensive magazine available. Packed full of articles, information, and health related products.

LIFE EXTENSION MAGAZINE
1881 Northeast 26 st. Suite 221, Wilton Manors, Fl 33305 (954)
561-8335 E-mail: LEmagazine@lef.org/ Url: http://www.lef.org
   A very practical magazine that covers both the traditional
and alternative medical fields. To keep up on the latest medical
and longevity information, this is a top-notch source.

WHOLE LIFE TIMES
P.O Box 1187 Malibu, CA 90265 (310) 317-4200
Url:http:www.wholelifetimes.com /E-mail: wholelifex@aol.com
   Today's most comprehensive holistic lifestyle journal. One
of the most respected magazines for content and cutting-edge
reporting. Full of new-age and holistic information.

ENERGY TIMES
2500 Grand Avenue, Long Beach, CA 90815-1764 (516) 777-7773
Url:http://www.energytimes.com / E-mail:
jgallo@naturesplus.com
   Enhancing your life through proper nutrition. This
magazine is packed full of the latest information, articles, and
products dealing with diet and nutrition. A must-read for those
interested in keeping up on the latest health developments.

INDEX

CONTACT, COMMENTS, AND CORRECTIONS

CONTACT THE AUTHOR AT:

Special Operations Consulting
1005 Banyan Drive
Virginia Beach, VA 23462 (877) 625-2653
E-Mail: janke@mindspring.com
URL: http://www.specopsconsulting.com

This book is updated each printing. If you have any comments, corrections or suggestions – please feel free to send them to the above address. If you would like to submit articles, information, or suggestions on the topics of self-discipline, personal achievement, success, nutrition, or any other self-improvement topics, please submit them at our website – http://www.specopsconsulting.com.

For a free subscription to our bi-weekly e-zine, Becoming SuperHuman, please e-mail us at our website. Articles for our e-zine can be submitted here as well.